Oscar,

I hope you find something useful here. Enjoy the book!

Living Well, Running Hard

Lessons Learned from Living with Parkinson's Disease

by

John Ball

John Ball
July 31, 2005

authorHOUSE™

1663 LIBERTY DRIVE, SUITE 200
BLOOMINGTON, INDIANA 47403
(800) 839-8640
WWW.AUTHORHOUSE.COM

First published by AuthorHouse 03/17/05

ISBN: 1-4208-2789-8 (sc)

Library of Congress Control Number: 2005900551

Printed in the United States of America
Bloomington, Indiana

This book is printed on acid-free paper.

Cover photograph by Action Sports International.

Table of Contents

Author's Note:

This work is drawn from personal memory. It is essentially true, but, of course, includes the occasional half-truth, misunderstanding, or unintentional mistake. Whenever possible, I tried to align my recollections with the facts, a much easier task when I could refer to the notes I had made about certain events at the time. Answers to some questions about time and place, outcomes and significance are still unclear. For example, when I recalled events from my childhood—the important ones I thought my family had shared—my siblings often had completely forgotten them, or remembered them differently. And most of the clever things I thought *I* had said or done were really said or done by my brothers or sister! Fortunately, the details of my childhood are not essential to this story, so I've eliminated, as much as possible, anything that happened before I turned 18. That's when, in the fall of 1962, I left my home in Lemon Grove, California for college in Seattle, Washington. From there on, I'm on safe ground with my version of the story, since no one was "tracking" me on a daily basis . . . and I preferred it that way for several years!

This book reflects my own opinions, biases, and interpretations of events. I included footnotes whenever I relied on the work of others for technical, scientific, or historical information.

Finally, this is not the complete story of my life but simply a set of stories about learning to live with Parkinson's disease. My friends have pointed out that I probably should wait to hear of someone's interest before I begin work on the sequel!

Acknowledgements

I would like to thank everyone who has helped me prepare this book for publication, particularly those who read it in the painful early stages of development. Since it has taken me nearly a decade to finish, I must start by thanking my wife and partner of more than thirty years, Edna. She has not only supported my running and writing over the years but she has read this manuscript in so many different stages that she probably knows much of it by heart. She has helped me in so many ways to deal with this disease that I'm not sure I could have completed either the book or the accomplishments it details without her. Second on that list would be Carol Walton, Executive Director of the Parkinson Alliance, and our guardian angel for Team Parkinson. She has provided extraordinary support and guidance for both the Team and this book. Among many others in the Parkinson's community, I would like to thank my fellow authors, Patti Leitner and Linda Herman. Their careful reading and helpful suggestions have gone a long way toward bolstering my resolve to get this book in print.

I would like to thank Steve Loizeaux, my good friend and long time co-worker. Steve's careful editing of the draft has helped make the book significantly more readable, and his thoughtful challenges to my stance on stem cell research have helped me define my own position more clearly. Steve and I are particularly concerned about the potential uses of stem cell technology because his wife, Barbara, lives with MS.

I would also like to thank all of you who have shared this long journey with me, particularly my running partners over the years: Tom Dean, Mike Carbuto, Gunnar Lindstrom, Mike Delgado, Aaron Yanagi, Mark Saxonberg, Doug MacGlashan and his wife Mimi, Dan Kiefer and all the members of the Honda Running Club and Team Parkinson. Without your encouragement, none of the benefits that I enjoy daily from running might have come my way.

Finally, I would like to dedicate this work and all the work my wife and I do for Team Parkinson to the memory of my mother-in-law, Chana Bialek. She lived her life with grace and faced her challenges with courage.

Chapter 1

The Discovery

I remember the night my future got a lot brighter. I was playing catcher on the company softball team one evening after work. The softball diamond was a brightly-lit pool of red earth and green grass in the surrounding darkness. The other team was wearing crisp blue uniforms with Motorola written boldly across the chest, while we wore an assortment of jeans, shorts, and red, white and blue tee shirts with a Honda Race Team logo on them. We couldn't get the company to spring for real uniforms like Motorola, but at least we got old race-team shirts for free! In spite of the usual enthusiasm and chatter of men at play, neither team was hitting well, so the game was excruciatingly slow. I was particularly frustrated with my own performance. It doesn't take much to play catcher in slow-pitch softball. You stand behind the plate and wait to catch the ball after it bounces on the mat for a strike, or lands off the mat for a ball. Then you retrieve it and throw it back to the pitcher. That's about all there is to the job. Once in a while you may also catch a desperate throw from the outfield, and make a diving lunge to tag out a runner barreling in from third. That happens maybe once or twice in a season. That night our pitcher, Larry Langley, hadn't found the range yet, and was putting lots of his pitches in the dirt. Our game was the last of four played that night, so the field was pretty torn up, making the balls bounce off at crazy angles. With each pitch, I had to wait for the ball to stop rolling before I could pick it up; my coordination

1

and balance were so poor that if I leaned over too quickly I would miss the ball or just fall over. I'd been having this trouble for several months, even when our game was the *first* of the evening, and the infield was smooth, and the grass had just been mowed.

I had once been a good athlete, though never a really good ballplayer. But now, in the summer of 1983, I was just a few months from turning forty, and losing it! While playing on this team for almost eight years, I'd gone from being a respectable outfielder with good range and a strong throwing arm, to what I was today, a really lousy catcher—a stumbling, fumbling wannabe who couldn't catch, couldn't hit, and couldn't even run to first base. I had failed as an outfielder, second baseman, and pitcher; catcher was the only spot left. Pitching was fun, but eventually I could no longer throw strikes. Now, as catcher, I couldn't even throw the ball back to the pitcher without bouncing it! They still let me swing the bat, but I'd lost so much mobility over the last year that someone else had to run for me if I happened to get a hit. The reason the team still let me bat was that they were consistently short of players and would have to forfeit games if they didn't have enough batters. That, and maybe the fact that I had been team manager for several years, was now the only reason I played at all.

But that night something changed. It was the third inning when Larry walked off the mound and asked, "What the hell is going on with you?"

"What do you mean? I'm trying my best..."

"Something's different about you tonight," Larry said. "You just threw the ball back to me three times in a row without bouncing it. That's the first time in months." He stared at me for a minute, then smiled and said; "You almost look like your old self."

I suddenly realized I *did* feel better, not as stiff or as awkward as usual. I could almost stand up straight. In fact, I felt almost human! Some of the team had come in to see what we were yakking about, and as I looked around at the other players' faces, I saw grins had replaced their usual pained looks of concern. Cranky old Ed Mazenko shouted from first base, "Hey John, what did you eat today, some magic beans?"

I reached into my jeans pocket, and took out the little packet of yellow tablets Dr. Beck had given me that morning. He had said, "Try these: one every four to six hours for a couple of days. If they do any good then maybe we'll know what you've got." No further explanation; nothing about what the pills might do or how I might react to them. Just take these and see what happens... a little like Alice in Wonderland! I had left his office in a bad mood that morning. I didn't like being used as a guinea pig. It wasn't the first time some doctor had tried that approach, and the first time had made me temporarily crazy. I mean really bonkers with terror and tears and feelings of hopelessness. I thought it was a poor way to make a diagnosis, like a mechanic just replacing parts until something finally works. I'd stuffed the pills into my pocket, and stalked out of the office. I waited until the end of the day to take the first tablet; I didn't want to risk going out of control at work like the first time. Now I looked again at the packet. What were these things anyway? The label said "Sinemet 25/100." I had no idea what that meant, but from where I was standing—with my head up and my shoulders back for the first time in months—they might as well have been labeled "magic beans". In the glare of that red earth infield, surrounded by the bright green outfield, the rest of the world didn't seem so dark any more. At home that night I pulled out my guide to prescription drugs, and looked up Sinemet. That's how I found out I had Parkinson's disease.

I was 39-years old, married nearly 10 years, and had two kids, David, five, and Sarah, three. When I read that Parkinson's disease affects more than a million Americans, I wondered why the doctors I'd been seeing for over 10 years had never even considered it. Then I saw why—people with Parkinson's are usually diagnosed in their 60's or later. Looking back over the years, I figured I'd shown symptoms of Parkinson's since I was about 27. Still, if someone had asked me how I felt at the moment I knew I had Parkinson's, I would have said I was a happy man. You may think that's an odd response to the diagnosis of an incurable, degenerative neurological disease! Yet for me it was such a relief to put a name to the problems I'd had all those years; I was no longer facing the unknown. There had been so many bad possibilities: -- a terminal brain tumor, or *coreo athetosis* or *myasthenia gravis* (that word *gravis* has too much of the word "grave" in it.) Finding out it was Parkinson's the way I did was also a relief because Sinemet, that miraculous little yellow tablet, relieved many of my worst symptoms.

I didn't know much about Parkinson's so I researched it during the next few weeks. A Scottish doctor named James Parkinson first described its characteristics in 1817. Before that it was simply called "shaking palsy". Not until 1960 did Austrian researchers Ehringer and Hornykiewicz discover that the primary cause of Parkinson's was the loss of dopamine-producing cells in the area of the brain called the *substantia nigra*.[1] Why those cells die is still unknown more than 50 years later. Dopamine is a neurotransmitter that enables signals to be sent back and forth through nerves between the brain and the body. It has to be in balance with another neurotransmitter, acetylcholine, for the brain to communicate effectively. Dopamine and acetylcholine are created in the brain, and in other parts of the body where they serve other functions. In Parkinson's disease, the dopamine-producing cells of the *substantia nigra* die out, eventually causing a severe communications breakdown. The cells that produce acetylcholine and other brain chemicals such as GABA, norepinephrine, and serotonin, may suffer only minor damage, but add to the wide array of Parkinson's symptoms. The brain is left unable to communicate effectively with the rest of the body. That's what caused me to lose my mobility, to wake up stiff and sore every morning, and to stand there, frozen in place, watching the softball slowly roll away.

Since dopamine is not difficult to manufacture, some doctors thought they might make up for any shortage in the brain by injecting it directly into the bloodstream, or giving it orally as a pill.

But the brain is practically isolated from the bloodstream. The cells in the walls of the brain's tiny blood vessels are packed so tightly that only very small molecules like glucose, oxygen, and

---

[1] Considerable additional information on Parkinson's disease is available from websites sponsored by the American Parkinson Disease Foundation, and the National Parkinson Foundation.

water can get through; dopamine molecules are much too large. This blood-brain barrier is actually a good thing because it maintains the right balance of chemicals for proper nerve function. It also keeps out bacteria, viruses, and most toxic substances, as well as hormones the brain puts *into* the bloodstream to control other parts of the body. So the brain must have sub-manufacturing units like the *substantia nigra* for everything it needs that can't get through the barrier.

When those dopamine producing cells in the *substantia nigra* die out, they aren't replaced by new ones. Until very recently, researchers thought that the brain stops creating new cells after infancy, and that adult brain cells never divide, and the brain can't regenerate them. Now they're not so sure. But without healthy living cells in the *substantia nigra*, there is no mechanism for keeping dopamine at the proper level in the brain. At least for now, once those cells are dead, you've got Parkinson's disease for life. Post-mortem examinations have shown most patients diagnosed with Parkinson's had lost 75 to 80% of their dopamine-producing brain cells by the time they were diagnosed.[2]

Even if you could continuously feed exactly the right amount of dopamine directly into the brain, you might be symptom free for a while, but you would still have Parkinson's. After all, those brain cells are dead, and the minute you stopped injecting the dopamine, or used too much, your symptoms would return. And it's not the same as hooking-up an insulin pump to your body to regulate the level of sugar in your blood. Without some way of getting dopamine to cross the blood-brain barrier, a pump would be useless.

In the early 1960's Dr. George Cotzias of New York discovered that levodopa, a chemical precursor of dopamine, can pass through the blood-brain barrier, and once in the brain, an enzyme (dopa-decarboxylase) converts it into useable dopamine. Although the levodopa (L-dopa in chemical shorthand) does get past the blood-brain barrier, it doesn't do it very efficiently. Dr. Cotzias found he had to give large oral doses of L-dopa to get even a small amount into the brain

---

[2] This information is available at many web sites dealing with neurological disease, including www.npf.org, www.wemove.org, and www.apdaparkinson.org/.

because most of it was being broken down while in the bloodstream. And any L-dopa that wasn't broken down caused significant side effects such as dyskinesia (involuntary random movements).

In 1969 Dr. Cotzias suggested that the levodopa needed a "partner compound" that could keep it from breaking down so quickly in the bloodstream. That led to the creation of a new molecule called carbidopa, a decarboxylase inhibitor that does the job. And fortunately, the carbidopa can't get past the blood-brain barrier where it could interfere with the conversion of levodopa to dopamine in the brain. So by reducing levodopa breakdown in the body, but not getting into the brain, carbidopa significantly increases the efficiency of levodopa, and reduces the dose required to get good results. This also reduces levodopa's unwanted side effects.

In the mid-1970's, levodopa and carbidopa were combined in a yellow, oval tablet called Sinemet that reached the market a few years later. When I was diagnosed with Parkinson's in1983, Sinemet had been in the market less than 10 years. After I began taking it, I could once again do all the physical activities I'd been missing. The diagnosis of Parkinson's and a prescription for Sinemet had given me back my life.

What now? I was at the mid-point of my life, having just come through a pre-mid-life crisis! So before going on with the second half, I wanted to take stock of the first. After a rocky start, I'd lived up to most of my parents' expectations, and hit many of the early targets I'd set for myself. My parents expected me and my siblings to go to college, but since they had very little money, we knew we were expected to pay our own way. After a lousy first couple of years in high school, I recovered just enough in my junior and senior years to become eligible for a couple of academic scholarships. And San Diego State had some interest in offering me a track scholarship. I wasn't exactly a track star, but most of the guys I competed with in high school were going away to major colleges on scholarships, so I was the kind of second-tier runner San Diego State could recruit at the time. I was pleased with their offer, but since my older brother was already a student at San Diego, I was eager to show my parents I could get into a major university. So, I kept looking.

Finally I managed to qualify for a Navy Hollowell scholarship to the University of Washington. It was a great opportunity for me to get away from my parents and the constant comparison to my older brother. It was that constant comparison and competition with my brother that sent me in the direction of the Navy scholarship. He had applied for the Hollowell program but failed the eye test during the physical exam. I was more fortunate on the physical. Jim was so good at being everything our parents wanted. I was somewhat lazy and immature, a prototype of the classic underachiever, although the term wasn't invented until a few years later. I hated doing high school homework, but enjoyed showing off my test-taking skills. Teachers disliked my attitude, and my grades suffered. High school track and cross-country running were my salvation, because everyone could see that I was willing to do the really hard work in training. My teammates might have been faster at the meets, but I was always challenging them in the workouts. That tenacity and competitiveness eventually carried over into my schoolwork; I realized I could just do the same thing in class that I did on the track. Be willing to do the busy work, not for the love of learning, but simply because my teachers expected it.

At the University I ran on the cross-country and track teams, but not under the scholarship program that supported the elite athletes. I was a typical "walk-on"—someone who really loved the sport, but wasn't good enough to recruit at a Division I school. I couldn't be counted on to bring in points in the big meets. In the winter of my sophomore year, what I thought were shin splints turned out to be a stress fracture in my left leg that went undiagnosed for several weeks. A blood clot formed around the fracture, which pinched off blood flow to my lower leg, and the calf muscle atrophied. The harder I trained, the worse it got. Once the coaching staff noticed my shrinking calf, they sent me to a specialist who found the clot and identified the stress fracture. I red-shirted my track season that spring.[3]

---

[3] The term "red-shirt" comes from the football team. Students who needed time to recover from injury or attend to their studies wore red shirts so they could practice with the team but not sacrifice their eligibility. The same rules applied to track, although we didn't actually wear red shirts.

I got hurt a few other times, and failed to make the traveling squad as a junior or senior. I did finally get healthy for the spring of my senior year, and managed to place second in a mile run at home against Washington State and Idaho, earning my "Big W" letter sweater. My time was around 4:18, but nobody had an accurate watch on me. Although it was the fastest mile I had ever run, it was not competitive at the university level. One of my own teammates at UW had run 4:05 twice that year, and Bob Day down at UCLA had run a 3:56! In some ways it was for the best, because I was very busy academically. The Navy expected all of us on the Hollowell scholarship to graduate in four years, whether or not we ran track or played football, or spent our time partying. I knew that I couldn't afford to be there without the scholarship money, so I had to get my degree in four years. That meant taking an average of 19 to 20 credit hours every quarter, because in addition to running and my degree requirements, I had to take Naval Science every quarter. I also added to my load by shifting my major from physics to English literature and creative writing in my sophomore year.

It all worked out, and I graduated from the UW in June of 1966 with a degree in English, and received my commission as a Naval Officer on the same day. A few days after graduation, I hitchhiked from Seattle to Pensacola, Florida to report for duty at the Naval Flight School. This story isn't about my brief career as a Navy pilot, so here's the "Cliff notes" version of it: I entered flight school in June of 1966, got my wings in August of 1967 and was asked to leave the service in February of 1971. I can't say my tour in the U.S. Navy was a success by conventional standards, but I did learn a great deal about myself, and the nature of war. After nearly two years in Southeast Asia, and a few scuffles with my superior officers about our role in the Vietnam conflict, I was happy to take their offer. I had severance money in my pocket, as well as a couple thousand hours of pilot time, my commercial pilot's license, an air transport rating and a flight instructor certificate. Best of all, I had a letter of thanks and an Honorable Discharge from my commission, signed by President Richard Nixon.

After the Navy, I toured Europe and Africa on a motorcycle, completed a Masters Degree at Cal State Los Angeles, found a good job, and married the woman of my dreams. Life was good! I felt fully engaged with it, in a happy swirl of family, friends, work and play. Any thoughts of an impending mid-life crisis, or losing much that I had gained because of Parkinson's disease, never occurred to me.

My life was blessed with good fortune...stable parents who loved each other, two brothers and a sister I could actually get along with— I no longer felt I had to compete with my older brother. I was doing well, and fully expected my life to continue that way. Why not? I did what I could to stay healthy and physically active— even in my first year in the Navy I had continued competitive running. I didn't cheat my employers, or ignore my family, and I lived a modest lifestyle. At 39, of course, my athletic career seemed like ancient history, but I had maintained an athlete's attitude, and worked at staying fit even though it became more and more difficult.

In my mid-20's, I began losing the constant urge to run, but not my urge to race. Where I was living may have had something to do with that: the Philippines and Viet Nam in the late 1960's were not ideal places to train for long-distance running! I occasionally jogged around the Navy base where I worked in the Philippines, but I wouldn't venture out on the roads. Who could guess what the Huks[4] or the Viet Cong might think of an American huffing along the road in a tank top and shorts? In Vietnam, running was definitely out. And when I returned to the States, only a few adults were in competitive running. They were the truly elite, Olympic-level runners like Marty Liquori and Jim Ryun trying to make a living on the Pro Track and Field circuit. Amateur runners depended on the backing of a few AAU clubs like the Bay Area Striders and the Boston Athletic Club. Though fond of running, I wasn't nearly good

---

[4] I served in the Philippines from March 1968 to November 1969. Under the Marcos regime in '68-69, a violent group of insurgents called the Huks supposedly lived in areas around U. S. military bases. I never actually met a Huk, or if I did I was treated with such courtesy that I never noticed.

enough to get club sponsorship. So for a few years I forgot about racing on foot, and concentrated on trying to go fast in airplanes, racecars and motorcycles. But I soon realized the skills that made me a good pilot didn't do anything for me as a racecar driver, and racing airplanes was way out of my price range. And racing motorcycles? You had to be "young and fearless," to be good, but since I was nearly 30, I rode more like "old and cautious." Luckily, my need for speed soon passed.

I stopped running competitively at about 23. Yet when I went back to school for my masters degree at 27, I reconsidered, thinking it would be easy to just start running again like I did in college the first time. But I was inconsistent and couldn't seem to make any headway. I always had nagging little problems that kept me off my training. This was frustrating because suddenly it became fashionable for adults to be seen in running shorts! At least some credit for that trend goes to a couple of guys who turned the marathon from an oddity into a cult by winning the Munich Olympics and the Boston Marathon.

Frank Shorter's victory in the 1972 Olympic Marathon was a major surprise, since no American had won an Olympic Marathon since 1904. Shorter, a graduate of Yale University—a school not known for its sports stars—was lightly regarded as a candidate for the gold medal. But he surprised everyone, running to a breakaway victory, and becoming an American hero. A few months later a local boy from Boston named Bill Rogers became the first American in more than a decade to win the Boston Marathon. By repeating his victory three more times over the next four years, he and Shorter created a cult around long-distance running. They never had much opportunity to compete head-to-head, but between the two of them, they raised the running consciousness of the whole country. Jim Fixx might also deserve some of the credit for this change. His book, The Complete Guide to Running,[5] introduced many new people to the discipline and joys of running. Then again, if I were a believer in conspiracy theories, I might want to credit the whole

---

[5] Fixx, James F., The Complete Book of Running, Random House, New York, 1977.

thing to Bill Bowerman, track coach at the University of Oregon during the 1960's and 70's. The University of Oregon dominated NCAA Track and Field during his tenure, creating such legends as Daryl Burleson, Jim Grelle, Steve Prefontaine and Alberto Salazar. He was a great coach who studied every aspect of running, and even built hand-made running shoes for his team. How did a small-town college track coach and part-time cobbler get linked up with world economic domination and conspiracy theorists? It was those hand-made track shoes! To market his new shoes, Bowerman created what would become an internationally dominant economic force: the Nike Shoe Company. Frank Shorter, Bill Rogers and Jim Fixx may have created an interest in running, but Nike created the market for running shoes, and eventually a lot more. They became an arbiter of fashion, a sponsor of professional athletes, and essentially killed the old notion of club-supported amateur athletics.

By the mid-1970's, adults everywhere were running. Men 40 and 50 years old were racing in 10k road races! Before the victories of Shorter and Rogers in Munich and Boston, the Boston Marathon had never had more than 500 entrants. But by the mid-70's, race organizers had to tighten the entry standards to keep the hordes of slower, unqualified runners from clogging the narrow Boston streets. In 1972 there were 124 marathons held in the US, but only six had more than 200 finishers.[6] By the mid-70's, many city marathons were drawing over 1000 entrants. Today, of course, the large city marathons like Chicago, New York and Los Angeles easily draw over 20,000 runners each. On average, 15,000 or more of them make it to the finish line. The New York City Marathon now draws over 40,000 runners every year, and applicants go through a lottery to get in.

What began as a change in attitude toward running became a shift in America's outlook on fitness in general. Fitness—especially jogging—was fashionable to talk about, and even do something about. Bill Bowerman, the same University of Oregon track coach that started Nike, brought jogging to America. Oddly enough, before

---

[6] Cooper, Pamela, The American Marathon, Syracuse University Press, Syracuse, NY, 1999, p. 120.

the 1970s jogging was not considered an exercise or sport. Bowerman had traveled to New Zealand and Australia to find out what made their middle distance runners—John Landy, Herb Elliott, Peter Snell, Rod Dixon and John Walker—so successful. In 1954, Landy was the second person ever to run a sub-four-minute mile, and he, Elliott (an Australian), Snell and Walker all held the world record in the mile over the next 20 years. The New Zealanders all trained under their national coach, Arthur Lydiard who was enormously popular not only because of his world-class athletes, but because he spoke to the average man and woman about the benefits of jogging. He believed you could get many of the benefits of running by merely jogging to raise your pulse rate. You could get in shape without trying to be competitive about it.

Bowerman realized that Lydiard's coaching methods not only produced record-setting middle distance runners, but also promoted a healthy, low-stress approach toward overall fitness. He returned to America with new ideas on how to teach middle distance runners, and with the message that you could be healthier without "pushing" yourself. Jogging caught on quickly once people realized you didn't have to beat yourself up to get in shape. When I stopped running in the mid-sixties, it was odd to see an adult male outdoors in running shoes and a sleeveless shirt. Ten years later, it was unusual to not have a pair of Nikes and split-thigh shorts in your closet. Like many other people, I had the shoes and shorts, but they didn't get much use. Cramps in my calves, and muscle spasms in my feet stopped me every time I went out to run.

Meanwhile, I finished my course work for a master's degree in English Literature at Cal State L.A. They didn't offer the comprehensive exam I needed to finish the degree that summer, so I decided to take a job for a few months while I studied for the fall exam. I found two jobs in two days. The first was in a photo studio, taking baby pictures. The second was a job at Kawasaki Motors as a technical writer to produce service bulletins, set-up instructions, and service manuals. I took the tech writing job. The work was fun, and included lots of photography to support the tech writing. I learned a lot about motorcycles as well as the publications business.

I loved photography. As a kid, I never had a camera of my own, and didn't get interested in either cameras or photography until I was in the Navy. I bought my first camera in Singapore, and soon began to "see" things differently. Then, on temporary duty from the Philippines to an assignment flying for the American Embassy in Djakarta, Indonesia, someone at the Embassy showed me how to develop and print my own film. That's what really hooked me, having such complete control over each image, from start to finish. For the next few years I was continually upgrading my camera equipment and buying darkroom equipment.

While attending Cal State LA, I set up a small darkroom in my bathroom. When I wasn't studying, I spent a lot of my free time printing different versions of the photos I'd taken in Asia, Europe and Africa. I was able to sell those photos from time to time, and that led me to set up a small photographic company with a friend in Hollywood. For the next two or three years, I wasn't sure whether I wanted to return to flying as a career, pursue technical writing, move into photography full-time, or continue my education. Tough decision! And I didn't want to eliminate any of those options: I liked to think I could succeed at any of them.

I can't remember any particular revelation—no blinding flash of light, or moment of spiritual awakening. It just slowly dawned on me that my life wasn't really complete. Not a bad life as it was, just not yet fully formed. That was in 1973 after working at Kawasaki for about a year. My age wasn't a problem, although I was nearly 30 and still single. It wasn't that I didn't know what I wanted—I wanted just about everything: to have both freedom and structure, to date anyone I fancied, to be with someone I loved, to have a job with purpose and value, and to come and go on my own schedule. I wanted to be creative and artistic, technical and scientific. There were just too many possibilities.

After high school my goal was to be a teacher. Now, I had completed my master's in English, and had my flight instructor's certificate, both of them qualified me to teach. After college my goal was to be a writer. And now as a tech writer, I had technical publications to my credit. When I left the Navy, I traveled by motorcycle with my camera, capturing beautiful images in Europe, Africa and North America. Finally, in the fall of 1973 I made three important decisions: buy a house in Santa Ana, California, return to graduate school at the University of California, Irvine, and . . . get married!

My decision to marry Edna was probably the easiest I'd ever made—I was ready to settle down. Many times I thought I had been in love, but I never felt ready for marriage. Not that I couldn't find anyone worth my long-term attention, I was just never quite finished with my own development. But when I met Edna, I was in a more comfortable place in life, living on my own terms, not driven by some unfinished assignment, and not obligated to anyone. That sense of freedom made it easy to make room for Edna in my life. She was fun, intelligent, and not demanding or insecure. I thought life would be far better with her than without her. Best of all, I was sure she loved me as much as I loved her because of the high price she was paying to be with me. Edna is Jewish, and I'm not. Her parents were survivors of the Holocaust. When she decided to date me, her parents shunned her, and she moved out on her own. When she decided to marry me, they cut her off completely. It was nearly 5 years before I met them.

We married on December 29, 1973, and moved to Santa Ana over the weekend. On Monday I went back to work at Kawasaki and also restarted my graduate studies at UCI. For the next few months I was a very busy man. The house we moved into in Santa Ana turned out to be a disaster. The floor furnace was broken, the water wouldn't flow from the street to the house, and a couple of electrical circuits were dead. This put my grad school studies in jeopardy; all my time was spent at work or at Angel's Hardware store, rather than the University library. But, after spending nearly every dollar we had on repairs, the house was finally safe to live in.

I soon realized though that something had to go. I was working six days a week at Kawasaki while still attending all my classes, so it was impossible to get all my writing assignments done for school. I was in Professor Tolliver's office one afternoon, explaining why I was going to be late with a paper, when he asked, "What would it take for you to get this paper done on time?" I said, "I suppose I'd have to quit my job and focus all my attention on my studies." He asked, "Would it help if I could offer you a teaching assistantship?" I told him, "Indeed it would!" With his help, I received a teaching position in the English Department . . . and I quit Kawasaki.

By the fall of 1974 we were settled into the house, and I was settling into my new job teaching Expository Writing. Once again, it seemed like a good time to get back into a solid fitness routine. I tried to run regularly, but it was just like before. I was constantly hit with leg cramps and muscle spasms in my left foot. There was also an overall stiffness that just never seemed to go away. One particularly painful cramping episode remains crisp in my memory even thirty years later

The tap water in Santa Ana tasted awful so we decided to buy bottled drinking water. The first time I hoisted one of the full glass bottles up to waist level; it slipped out of my hand and crashed down on my bare left foot, crushing the middle segment of my big toe. It hurt like hell! After a couple of hours it was so swollen and painful I had Edna take me to the University health center. They x-rayed it and agreed that I had not only broken it, but squashed it flat. So they wrapped a piece of adhesive tape around it, and sent me home with a handful of painkillers. There was nothing more to be done with a broken big toe. A few days later, walking across the UCI campus, my foot began to spasm just like it normally did after a short walk. But this time, all the strength in my foot was trying to curl that broken toe under my arch. It literally brought me to my knees. I knelt there in the grass and cried for nearly a quarter of an hour until the cramp finally eased. Once I stopped whimpering and could stand up again, I decided to skip class, and headed for the University health center once more. This time they sent me to a neurologist at a large local hospital.

Dr. Alston performed several tests over the course of a week, but wasn't certain what was wrong. He eventually came up with a tentative diagnosis of *correo athetosis*, which he described as "localized epilepsy" affecting a small portion of my brain. He prescribed Valium to dampen the excess activity in my brain; I tried it, but couldn't feel any improvement. The Valium didn't change the frequency or intensity of the spasms. I didn't really trust the doctor's diagnosis or his treatment for it, so I gave up on Valium, and tried again to work around the problem.

Since I couldn't run with any regularity, I replaced my running program with handball and racquetball. That reduced the cramping episodes in my left foot, but I could still feel that something was wrong. I loved to play full bore, but once I tired a little, my shoes seemed to stick to the court floor as if someone had spilled a coke on it. I just couldn't pick up my feet. And when I had to backpedal for a deep shot, I found it impossible to stop until I bumped against the back wall. I assumed it was a question of conditioning, and I just needed to work a little harder at it. But no matter how hard I worked, I could tell I wasn't getting any better.

This "inconvenience" slowly became more troublesome. Whenever I got tired, I developed a shuffle, or stutter-step. I began rocking in place whenever I tried to stand for a long time. People began to worry that I was drinking too much, when in fact, I rarely drank at all. And the spasms on my left side were occurring more often. These symptoms didn't develop all at once, but gradually, over months and years.

My new teaching job, along with the money I received from the GI Bill, actually gave me a pay increase over what I was making at Kawasaki. Our lifestyle took another step up when Edna landed a job. We not only had more money, but I had more time. I stayed in grad school for just over two years, and loved nearly all of it. The English Department at UCI was on a mission to become the center of a new movement in the study of literature, called contextualist theory. The presence of such luminaries as Hazard Adams and Murray Krieger had attracted some of the brightest young literary minds to their graduate program. In my seminars, surrounded by the most intelligent young hotshots in the academic world, I sometimes felt out of place. In fact I felt old. I was a Vietnam vet, over 30, and married. Although for several years I had planned to finish my Ph.D. and teach English at the university level, I began to see that the academic world is very competitive, and I would be hard pressed to keep up with these kids.

After nearly two years of trying to keep up, my doctoral studies were beginning to flag. Except for one class, I had completed my coursework in reasonably good shape. But I was dreading the work necessary to prepare for my oral exams. And the requirement for two foreign languages posed a challenge; my last foreign language course was German, as a freshman in college. To my surprise, I passed a German translation course at UCI with some dexterity, just on the strength of that one college course and three years of German in high school. But I still needed another language and I would have to learn it from scratch. The only intensive language class available was a summer class in conversational Italian. I had no desire to learn Italian, but I had to try it. Unfortunately, I failed the class on the first attempt, and had to repeat it the following year, which meant another summer of being called "Giovanni Testicolo." Fortunately, I passed the final translation assignment, a passage from Dante. It wasn't enough to translate Italian; it had to be 14th century Italian at that!

I probably wasn't highly regarded by my committee professors, even though I had selected them because they were genuine experts in my subject areas. I had figured out my problem, but it was going to be difficult to solve. My approach to literature was mismatched with the prevailing philosophy of the department. The professors in the English department at UCI were leading the charge into contextualist theory, and I was an archetypal reader. I think I understood what they were driving at, but it wasn't what I wanted to get out of literature. I would have been better off studying with Northrop Frye or Joseph Campbell, who were the leading lights of archetypal criticism. One contextualist professor at UCI was so offended by my analysis of Don Quixote, that he gave me a C+ for both the paper and the class. Although the professor was not on solid ground with his own work, and was soon dismissed from the department, that C stayed on my transcript. A single poor grade wouldn't drop a student from the doctoral program, but it did cost me my teaching assistantship. Without the income from the teaching, Edna and I were back on budget lectures with zero in the entertainment account. I still wanted to finish the degree, but the challenge seemed to be growing more difficult.

Edna and I shared a busy life. Since her family had not accepted our marriage, most of our activities were built around my family and our mutual friends from work. Our move to Santa Ana to be near UCI had forced her to find a new job, and she went to work for an industrial hardware firm, handling sales accounts over the phone. We had developed a network of social contacts through my sister Eileen (nicknamed Kippi) and her husband Mike who introduced us to the BMW Automobile Club—they had become familiar with the then obscure European brand when Mike's brother brought a small 2-liter BMW sedan back from Europe. Mike's brother drove the car incredibly fast, and Mike grew to love BMWs. When the BMW 2002 was introduced in the U.S., Mike was among the first to buy one in early 1968. My father followed his lead a few months later and bought the 1600cc version. When I returned home in November of 1969 after nearly 2 years in Asia, I needed a car, and had planned on getting a Porsche with the money I'd saved. But when I realized I could go just as fast, use less gas, and save some money, I bought a BMW too! It was dark blue, and came with a sunroof and am-fm radio, all for about $3700—a good deal at the time. So, along with Mike and Kippi, Edna and I qualified for the BMW club, whose members were a close-knit group of young married couples with an interest in car racing and BMW products. Edna wasn't interested in competitive driving, but she enjoyed the social side of the club. I attended a couple of the driving schools, and competed in several slaloms, rallies and some road racing. I enjoyed the competition, in spite of being mediocre in the actual races, but I did well in the more precision-oriented rallies. I also enjoyed working on the car: I installed several modified parts to improve its performance, and to keep it running as things began to wear out due to the high mileage I was accumulating. I was happy to find that the hands-on skills I learned from my Dad were still there. I knew of only one other teaching assistant in the English department at UCI who could repair his own car, and the two of us often laughed about that.

By mid-1975 I was restless. I was making little progress on my dissertation and preferred to spend my energy with the students in my writing class. The students were usually bright kids, but unfortunately, many of them did not understand even the fundamentals of thinking, let alone writing. Teaching them to express their thoughts clearly was a big challenge. The university didn't require assistants to be trained in the art of teaching, so I found myself struggling to reach my students. I tried various approaches, including using photographs in class as the subject matter for writing assignments. Some of the students just sat there, unable to connect the photos with any coherent thought. One young female student looked at me and whined, "But they're just pictures." I felt like grabbing her by the shoulders and shouting, "Yes! That's the point! They are pictures, and each one is easily worth a thousand word essay!" I never got through to some of them.

Occasionally it was the instructor, not the students, who just didn't get it. One student in particular brought this message home to me. He was from an inner-city high school in downtown LA, brought up in a racially-mixed family, with a Philippine mother who spoke Tagalog at home, and a black father who was mostly absent. He was struggling a little in my Writer's Workshop, a euphemism for "Bonehead English," designed for people who didn't meet the University of California's minimum standards SAT score. Many students who were otherwise highly qualified for the University were quite weak in their writing skills. In Ty's case, he was clearly bright and charming, but needed to pay more attention to his use of language. Since English was not his first language, I asked him if his high school had classes in English as a second language. He said, "Yes. I was one of the best tutors."

He came to my desk one afternoon just before my official 'office hours.' I was finishing up a game of chess with a fellow grad student, and enjoying a victory. When I finished the game, Ty asked if he could play me. Thinking I could finish the game before my office hours started, I said, "Sure." It didn't take long, all right, but it didn't go quite as I expected. Before I could even figure out what his opening gambit was, Ty quickly captured several of my major pieces, including my bishops, one rook, and both knights. I could see that my queen was threatened as well. I looked at the situation, saw it was hopeless, and decided to resign the game. Ty looked at me with a smile and said, "You shouldn't give up so easily." Then he turned the board around and quickly beat me with the few pieces I had left. I had badly underestimated him, and I suddenly realized I might have done the same with many of my students simply because they couldn't express themselves clearly in writing. Intelligence is not evenly distributed in people; they can be bright in one area and dull in another. That insight has guided my thinking ever since.

Chapter 2

Getting Back to Work

In January, 1975, I got a call asking if I could help the Bob Bondurant Driving School with a new car introduction. I had met Bondurant at a BMW Club-sponsored driving school at Ontario Motor Speedway a few months earlier. I was between quarters at school, so I took the job. It was the press introduction of Honda's new Civic CVCC. The people I worked with on that event were energetic and friendly. They put in long days, but appeared to have a lot of fun doing it. What I remember most was that they let us drive the cars to the limit!

The guys from our BMW Club were all working at the "fuel economy" station, and we could see that the cars got really excellent mileage. But to get those big mileage numbers, the press people were driving the cars at a snail's pace around that lovely 2-½ mile oval. Once the press was all through, we took the cars out to see just how good they were at the other end of the driving scale. We knew they could get better than 50 miles per gallon if you drove them very conservatively, but we wanted to know how fast they could go. One little Civic by itself could just about make 95 mph flat out around the banked track. But when we got two of them nose-to-tail, it went up to 96. By the time we had five of them in a tight little line with no more than a foot or two between them, we topped out at almost 100 mph. Nobody from Honda came over to tell us we had to stop. In fact, I think they were as curious as we were—they seemed unhampered by conventional thinking or the constraints of company policy. So when I received an offer later that year to work as a technical writer on a special project for Honda, the timing seemed perfect. It would give me a break from my studying, and give me a chance to think about my thesis. Perhaps with a little time away from school, I could come up with a fresh way of looking at John Milton's <u>Paradise Lost</u>. So, I took a yearlong leave of absence from graduate school. I thought I could finish the project in a year and get back to my dissertation on Milton, but the project turned out to be a more exciting assignment than I expected. After a year of working in the fast-paced, high volume environment at Honda, the thought of returning to a dissertation on a 500-year-old poem seemed silly. Instead of returning to school to complete my exams and dissertation, I decided to stay with Honda. Since then the car business has been the center of my work life.

My physical challenges continued, but were fortunately more of an inconvenience than a limitation. I couldn't walk across the Honda parking lot in Gardena without getting a cramp in my left foot, but I had no problem crawling all over the cars we worked on. We spent long days sorting out repair procedures, and taking step-by-step photographs as we disassembled prototype cars and put them back together. It was a fun job, and I was working with some very bright and motivated people, particularly my boss Charlie Black, and the technical trainer, Lewis Prator. Lewis didn't say much, but he had a way of letting you know when you needed to go back to the car and figure things out again. He had me take things apart and put them back together several times, until I was comfortable with Honda's unusual technology. The entire auto service division was located in one room of the corporate headquarters in Gardena, California. The majority of the staff in Gardena concentrated on the motorcycle business, and the automotive group was probably no more than a couple hundred people. They had a real "can-do" spirit, and no budget—they simply spent money as they needed it.

I joined the softball team as a way of integrating myself into American Honda culture. I played in the outfield the first year, but was moved from right field to second base as my mobility declined.

By the third year I was moved to the pitcher's mound, where I tried my best for a couple of years. Our team's fortune went up and down. Every time we had a good season, the league office would move us up from the D league to C or even B level, where we'd get our butts soundly trounced for a year or more. But we always found a way to get better as the competition got stiffer, just like we did in the car business. Unfortunately, as our team got better, I got worse. Finally, I had to move to catcher because I could hardly move at all. The team continued to let me play, but I was limited to standing behind the plate, waiting for the ball to stop moving before I could pick it up. If I tried to pick it up before it stopped bouncing or rolling, I usually stumbled or fell. If I played on offense, it was just to swing the bat, and if I actually hit the ball they'd send a substitute runner. Through it all, I continued seeking medical help, but each doctor I saw had a different interpretation of the symptoms.

I was referred to a doctor in Whittier named Pirandozzi. He was a well-known cardiologist who had worked on a similar cramping problem for the mile world-record holder, John Walker of New Zealand. Walker was the first runner in the world to break 3:50 in the mile, and was the gold medalist at the 1500-meter in the 1976 Montreal Olympics. Like me, he was having cramps in his feet, and had seen several doctors before being diagnosed with a circulation problem that restricted the blood flow through his calf muscles. The explanation was that he had trained so hard that the muscles of his legs outgrew the sleeve of tissue around them and pinched off the arterial blood flow. The doctor cut the sheath around Walker's calf muscles to allow the blood to flow more freely. I believe a similar treatment was applied to Mary Decker Slaney, allowing her career to be extended significantly. I'm not sure it helped in Walker's case—his racing career wound down over the next three or four years.[7] In my case, the treadmill tests showed normal circulation even with the muscle spasms in progress, so I wasn't a candidate for that treatment. The cardiologist referred me to a neurologist named Beck, also in the Whittier area, and I worked with him through a

---

[7] According to fellow runner Steve Scott, John Walker was diagnosed with Parkinson's disease about 1996, and lives quietly in New Zealand.

series of CAT scans, spinal taps, and treadmill tests until we were exhausted with each other.

In May of 1977, Edna was working at a company in the City of Industry, just north of Whittier, and I was tired of the long commute from Santa Ana to Gardena. Since I'd been working with doctors around Whittier, and Edna's office was near there, we found a new home in the west end of Whittier, not far from the freeway. It was a much nicer place with three bedrooms and a large living room and kitchen, and the location cut nearly half-an-hour off my commute. The house was fairly new, but built in an older neighborhood on a lot that had been vacant nearly 30 years. The neighbors on both sides were very nice and had been there for some time. The community was also a nicer place to raise children than our small crowded home in decaying Santa Ana. Around the time we moved to Whittier, I followed up with Dr. Beck. I would never accuse this doctor of jumping to conclusions, because we went over ground that I thought we had thoroughly covered before. He looked for, but found no evidence of a brain tumor or damaged spinal cord. We repeated the CAT scans, which clearly showed normal brain structure, and a second spinal tap didn't produce any new information. With no other ideas in mind, he referred me to an orthopedic surgeon who had treated other athletes with similar cramps and spasms in their lower limbs.

Even through this time of uncertainty about my health, Edna and I were feeling good about our relationship and comfortable in our new home. I also felt good about my job and about Honda, so Edna stopped taking the "pill." It took a while for her to get pregnant the first time, but we had fun trying, and eventually had two children, David in 1978 and Sarah in 1980. And boy did our life change after that! We referred to life before David and Sarah as "BC," or Before Children. After they came along, we didn't know what to call it.

His Parkinson's is evidently more severe than mine, and progressing more rapidly. Additional information regarding Walker's condition is available in: "The Interview – John Walker: ... Simon Turnbull talks to the 'Flying Kiwi' ahead of his big London reunion." 03 August 2003, posted by Murray Charters <mcharters@novus-tele.net>

David and Sarah each made their entrances in their own way. David was a challenge from the first. Edna was healthy throughout the pregnancy, but as typical first-time parents, we reacted, or overreacted, to every little change along the way. We prepared as best we could, attending childbirth classes, painting the baby's room, and buying baby furniture. I even built a cradle in an adult woodworking class at a nearby high school. We also began a series of breakthrough meetings with Edna's extended family. Edna worked at her job right up to two weeks before her due date, and the day after she stopped working, we went to visit her Aunt Bluma and Uncle Max for the first time. We had a very nice dinner, and I felt comfortable with her aunt and uncle, in spite of the fact that we had been together nearly five years before I was even allowed to meet them. As we were leaving the house that evening, Edna missed a step, no more than an inch of concrete between the porch and sidewalk, and fell heavily on her very pregnant belly. Everything seemed okay, even though we were all a little shaken by the fall.

Later that night Edna woke me up and said she was in labor. She'd been through one set of false labor pains a few weeks earlier, so I was skeptical at first, but when they persisted, we grabbed the pre-packed bag and drove off to Kaiser Hospital in Bellflower. We went through all the admitting procedures and everything looked good, but each time the doctor came in and checked Edna's dilation, it was stuck at 5 cm. She continued having labor pains at regular intervals, but the dilation process was stalled. This dragged on for hours. Finally, with Edna's blessing, I left the hospital to get some rest, but she got no rest at all. Hour after hour, she huffed and puffed, but nothing changed. They decided to help her along with Pictosin, a synthetic form of oxytocin, the natural hormone that stimulates contractions. They had attached a fetal monitor to check on the slow progress the baby was making, and as the Pictosin increased the force of each contraction, the monitor became very erratic. When the baby's pulse dropped off the chart completely, I ran for the doctor, but couldn't find anyone at first because they were going through a shift change! I was nearly in a panic by the time a nurse explained that the monitor had simply come loose from the baby, and everything was okay.

Finally, 21 hours after we arrived at the hospital, David Thomas Ball was born on Halloween afternoon. He was roughed up by the delay, his feet were blue, and his head was very pointy, but we thought he was beautiful. When placed in the weighing scale, he did a sort of push-up, raising his head to look around as if thinking to himself, "So this is my new place…Well, you all had better get ready for some changes."

After a couple of days, Edna was ready to leave the hospital, but David had turned slightly yellow with jaundice, and needed to be kept one more night. Since Edna was trying to breast feed, she felt uncomfortable leaving him, even for one night, but she was glad to get home. We returned early the next morning to find David lying in a little clear-plastic crib, in his bright blue diaper and little eye-patches, basking in the light from the special sun lamps. He looked like a California Surfer baby, ready for beach blanket bingo!

The nurse came over and cautiously asked, "Is this your baby?"

The tone in her voice immediately set off a warning signal in my brain.

"Yes, this is our son. Why do you ask?"

She spoke slowly, choosing her words carefully. "Well, there's something I have to tell you about your son. He's got a very strong will, and will be quite a challenge to raise I'm sure."

"What do you mean? Doesn't that have a lot to do with the way we raise him?"

She stood there for a moment, then smiled and said, "Well, I've been a pediatric nurse for 25 years, and if he can get his way with me, when he's got no language skills and only two days experience in this world, what chance have you got?"

She was right of course.

Sarah was the opposite. She arrived about 16 months later, on March 1, 1980 with minimal inconvenience, at Whittier Presbyterian Hospital. Labor was brief and the delivery easy. She's been just as trouble-free ever since. When the obstetrician, Dr. Deasy, saw that it was a girl, he said, "Well, now you have one of each, you can stop while you're behind." He offered to tie off Edna's reproductive capability right then, but we weren't ready to make that decision just yet.

The children helped us reunite Edna with her family. The process had started a few years before David was born, when Edna's mother, Chana, was hospitalized with a broken hip. The fall was serious, and her mother's health had been deteriorating for years after being diagnosed with Parkinson's disease at age 48, when Edna was 11. Because of the PD, Chana had a tendency to fall, and because of her reduced mobility and consequent weight gain, her bones were brittle. Peter Bialek, Edna's father, had told Edna not to visit or call them, but one of her cousins kept her informed of family events. But this was too serious to ignore, so Edna went to see her mother in the hospital.

At first she tried to go when her father was not there, but that was just too inconvenient, so, in her mother's hospital room, they met face-to-face again for the first time nearly three years after we were married. They barely spoke, and for a time Peter still refused to accept Edna back into the family. Her mother came around far more quickly, and the mother-daughter relationship was easily mended. But Peter struggled; until he found out she was pregnant with David. A grandchild on the way was something to be proud of, and this would be a Jewish baby, because Jewish birthright is passed through the mother, not the father.

When David's Jewish circumcision took place in November of 1978, our entire family surrounded the rabbi: Bialeks and Balls, as well as Peters, Gryczman, Stolz and many more. My father, whose role was minimal in the ceremony, nearly passed out when the *Mohel* made the cut. David's godparents, John and Elaine Everson were also in town for the event. John didn't look especially Jewish, even with his *yarmulke* covering the thinning spot on his blond head, but he looked more than a little pleased to share the experience with Edna and me.

On another front, checking over my Pilot's logbook shows a big gap in my flight time beginning in 1978. There are two reasons really: first, the birth of our son and second, my escalating physical challenges. As my ability to walk and run declined, I gradually cut back on my flying, even though I didn't feel like it affected me in the cockpit. After all, I didn't feel like I needed to stop driving, or riding motorcycles, so why shouldn't I fly? I tried to convince myself the reduced flight time was due to my busy work and school schedule, but it honestly had more to do with my uncertain medical condition. I was losing confidence in my body. When I left the Navy, I had a full range of pilot certifications, including an Air Transport rating in the DC-3, a Certified Flight Instructor rating, and an Instrument Flight Instructor rating. And I had worked as an instructor on weekends during my first year in graduate school. But by early 1979 my future as a pilot was in doubt. I did pass my annual flight physical but I didn't talk about some of the problems I was having with my balance and my ability to move backward. The doctor may have noticed something, but he couldn't see any reason to ground me. So I grounded myself.

In 1979 I went to see Dr. Waggoner, the orthopedic surgeon recommended by Dr. Beck. He had treated a patient with similar pain and leg cramps, and successfully restored function with surgery, by removing muscle pressure on the sciatic nerve. He thought pressure from the piriformis muscle on my left side could be causing the problem. We discussed the possibility, and his explanation made some sense. He examined my sciatic nerve by pressing on it in an embarrassing, as well as painful, anal exam. It was a convincing demonstration that the nerve was inflamed, and lacking any more reasonable approaches, I agreed to the surgery. The procedure required a cut of nearly 15 inches in my buttock to pull apart the layers of muscle to reach the piriformis muscle. According to the doctor, the nerve had been severely pinched because it passed through the muscle, rather than around it. He said the nerve appeared quite flattened and inflamed, so to relieve the pressure on it he trimmed away part of the muscle. After a brief recovery in the hospital, I went home on crutches. Within a few days after coming home, I tried walking around the block on my crutches, and the spasm in my foot returned almost immediately. The surgery had proven completely ineffective.

After about 8 weeks at home recovering from the surgery, I returned to work, and tried to forget about doctors for a while. So far, none of them had been able to help me. Even after the surgery, *nothing had changed.* When I returned to work, I got an opportunity to move on from the Service Manual project in Publications to a new position in Service Training. I had spent a lot of time working with the trainers to develop information on new model vehicles, and they liked my work, so I was offered a promotion to write curriculum for dealer technicians. I jumped at the chance to get back into an educational role, this time with the title of Instructional Designer (ID). As soon as I got the title, I decided to learn what an instructional designer does! Luckily, my new boss, Dr. Tom Dean, was a professional educator, and he gave me the opportunity to learn my new job responsibilities. Tom was also a runner, and a hiker. I wanted to run and hike with him, but for the time being, I had given up on running and hiking, and on doctors.

Recovery from the surgery was slow, and two or three years later I was so frustrated with my condition that I started seeking out doctors once more. Since the traditional Western approach to medicine had failed, I tried getting relief from acupuncture, but it also proved useless. By early 1983 I was in such discomfort all the time that I went back to Dr. Beck, the neurologist. I reminded him that it was his idea I see Dr. Waggoner, but he just shrugged it off like it had nothing to do with him. By this time he could see that my symptoms were far more pervasive than they had been. But even with more obvious symptoms to work with, he still could not identify a precise cause. I was discouraged. My elbows and knees felt like ratchet mechanisms had replaced the smooth joints. They clicked and jerked as I tried to move them. I was stiff all over, and felt awkward all the time now. But I was still fit and strong because through it all I had kept up a fairly rigorous exercise routine. The doctor was baffled, because I could still do a lot of physical tasks quite well. Perhaps my overall fitness masked some of the seriousness of my disability.

Out of ideas again, Dr. Beck referred me to a specialist in *myasthenia gravis.* I was more than a little nervous, because I had just read a novel in which the main character died of the disease. The specialist did an extensive medical exam, and although he could see several symptoms similar to those of myasthenia, he was still uncertain. He explained that one way to find out would be to prescribe a new drug that was recently developed to treat the condition, and if it helped, then myasthenia was most likely the problem. It seemed to me a rather unscientific approach to diagnosis, but knowing that medicine is sometimes more art than science, I went along.

Unfortunately, I had to leave on a business trip right after seeing the doctor, so I called Edna from the airport to tell her I still had no diagnosis. We were anxious about the possible outcome of the visit, and we wanted to be together if/when a diagnosis was confirmed. But business took priority, and I left on the trip as scheduled. I took the first dose of the drug shortly before heading into a major business meeting, and rather than making me feel better, it made me crazy! Within an hour of taking the first pill, I felt as nutty as a fruitcake. I felt utterly alone. I was suddenly overwhelmed with emotion, terrified, and I began to weep, right there in the meeting. I had suddenly become afraid, afraid of being sick, and afraid of dying. After tearfully clinging to one of my associates for a minute or two, while the others looked on in wonder, I excused myself from the meeting, went back to my hotel room, collapsed on the bed and wept. It was a devastating experience; I'm just thankful that when the medication wore off, the fear and anxiety went with it. Clearly, I didn't have *myasthenia gravis*. I was relieved to eliminate one more potentially fatal disease, but still no closer to understanding my condition.

Having no other options, I returned once more to Dr. Beck. More poking and probing followed, but the condition remained a mystery. Finally, out of frustration, I suspect, the doctor shoved a sample of yellow tablets into my hands on my way out the door, and said, "Here, see what these do for you." Again, I was annoyed by such an unscientific approach, but I wasn't in a position to argue with him. I needed help. I took the first tablet shortly before driving to a softball game and ... well; you know the rest of that story.

When I went back to the doctor a few days later and told him how well this new medication worked, he was skeptical, but he saw the objective evidence. I could perform all the usual tests much better than just a few days earlier. I was 39 and had been struggling with these problems for 12 years, and yet a single tablet produced an incredible response. Since Sinemet was only prescribed for one condition, Parkinson's disease, he cautiously diagnosed me with "Parkinson's syndrome" or "parkinsonism." I think he was reluctant to say with any certainty that I had Parkinson's disease, because, in his experience, Parkinson's was a disease of old age. Later, I realized this was probably because his experience was just too limited. I don't think he had ever heard of the "young onset" phenomenon, but then, maybe that term hadn't even been suggested yet.

It seems odd to me now, but I don't remember making any connection immediately between my condition and that of Edna's mother, Chana. Of course her Parkinson's and mine weren't linked genetically. But I didn't even stop to think what Edna must feel like; watching her mother suffer quietly with PD for more than fifteen years already, and then being told that her husband had the same disease. I was just happy I could once again walk across the parking lot at work without setting off a spasm in my foot, and stand still without looking like a drunk on a binge.

Shortly after I started taking Sinemet regularly, Edna and I celebrated our tenth anniversary by taking a cruise. We left David and Sarah with my parents near San Diego, and sailed off to Mexico just before Christmas of 1983. On the cruise ship I made a fool of myself by trying to do aerobics with the ship's instructor. In every picture Edna took, I'm completely out of step with the rest of the group, but at least I was in there, trying to keep up. I played tennis, went for a parasail ride in Puerto Vallarta, and even ran on the beach at Acapulco. I was happy to be celebrating ten years of marriage, and almost as happy with the return of my physical capabilities. I trusted our marriage completely, but it took a while to get that confidence in my body back after all those years.

Not being able to run had been difficult for me, as I suspect it would be for anyone when the reality of your life is out of synch with the image inside. I'd spent many hours in doctors' waiting rooms, waiting to be poked, stuck, measured, and scanned. I had limped along on treadmills with my toes curling up under my foot, and electrodes attached all over my body, but for 12 years the problem remained a mystery. Through it all, I still thought of myself as a runner. Then, after all the frustration, pain and fear, I was diagnosed with Parkinson's disease. I don't think my journey to that diagnosis could be described as either good science or effective medicine, but I'm thankful it ended in relief. It enabled me to once again integrate my body image with the physical reality. Sinemet let me move without difficulty, and I began to run again in the early months of 1984. Finding out I had Parkinson's had given me my life back.

Chapter 3

Family Secrets

When I was diagnosed with PD, Edna insisted we keep it a secret from her mother and father. They were Holocaust survivors, after all, and had suffered so much. Why burden them with something more to worry about? They already knew how terrible a disease Parkinson's was. Chana had suffered from it since the mid-1960's. She was diagnosed before Dr. Cotzias had discovered levodopa, and had been living with the disease for nearly ten years before Sinemet was created. Her husband Peter was part of the old school: you dealt with illness internally, and kept it in the family. He became her personal attendant and caregiver, but also pulled her out of routine interaction with society. Let me say that his was not an unusual response. Until the development of Sinemet, Parkinson's was an "invisible" disease because once diagnosed, most people retreated from life. It was just too embarrassing, too difficult to get about, and too hard on those who loved you to see you like that.

By the time I met her, Chana was taking Sinemet and maybe other Parkinson's medications and she managed to get around with a walker for a few years. But over time, her ability to stand and walk on her own declined significantly. Peter didn't want her to be seen in a wheelchair, or maybe he didn't want to be seen pushing her about, so she got out less and less. She spent most of her day at home in her recliner chair, and grew weaker, and therefore when she tried to get up, she often fell. With the inactivity and loss of muscle tone, her bones became more fragile, and over the years she broke both her hips, and her arms. Chana didn't like being stuck in that chair all day, but Peter and Edna didn't want her to get hurt. They constantly told her she should not get up without help. In their eagerness to protect her, they imprisoned her in the chair.

Peter had to take care of many things, like getting Chana to and from the bathroom, cooking dinner, and hundreds of other chores. The way they chose to deal with the disease placed a great deal of stress on the entire family. So it's easy to understand Edna's reluctance to tell them I had Parkinson's. Even if I had been free to discuss the Parkinson's with my mother-in-law, it would have been difficult. I could barely hear her when she spoke, and she tended to speak in a mixture of English, Yiddish and Polish. A faint voice is characteristic of people living with PD, because the muscles that operate the vocal cords are affected just like other muscles of the body.

Looking back at that situation, I wonder how Edna was able to face my diagnosis in light of her mother's experience. True to my character, I don't even remember asking what she thought, or how she felt. Perhaps the bigger secret she had to keep was not hiding my diagnosis from her family, but hiding her fears from me. Was it possible for her to see my future in different terms than her mother's experience? Or did she imagine I would face the same shrinking access to the world? And that she would have the same increasing responsibilities for my day-to-day care as her dad did for her mom?

When I started running again, it was only a couple of days a week, but as the strength and fluidity returned to my arms and legs, and my cardiovascular system began to catch up, my thoughts turned toward racing on the roads. It never occurred to me to wonder why I wanted to compete. I'm competitive by nature, it's not a choice. I am, therefore I compete, end of story. Just before turning forty, I started entering 5k runs. In my third race at a small, local event at Legg Lake near the Whittier Narrows in California, I ran 22 minutes, 50 seconds, and placed third in my age group. People around me had no idea why I whooped so loudly for a lousy third place medal in a sparsely attended race in the park. You would have thought I won the lottery. At least Edna, David and Sarah were with me, and they seemed quite proud of Dad. From then on I was hooked on road racing. I scanned the papers for local races, and tried to enter at least one each month. I punched up the frequency of my workouts to four or five times a week, but probably averaged no more than 15-18 miles a week at best. It was fun, and even though I was still facing some challenges, I felt comfortable competing with those in my age group. Those little yellow "magic beans" put me on an equal footing with the rest of the world.

One evening in early November of 1984, I was attending a parents' meeting at my son's grade school, when I noticed the guy next to me was wearing the rattiest looking running shoes I had ever seen. I introduced myself, and he said his name was Mike Carbuto. I told him I admired his shoes because they looked like they had lots of miles behind them. He laughed, and said he ran a lot of marathons. I was stunned. He seemed to be in his mid-thirties, and was not particularly athletic looking: rather short, a little heavy, and somewhat bow-legged. His shoes were worn extremely thin on the outside edges, like misaligned tires on a car. I wasn't sure whether to take him seriously or not. He said, "I'm going to be running down in Long Beach on Sunday morning. Why don't you come down and join me? We can run a 10K together."

I'd been running alone, and thought it would be good to find a local running partner, so I agreed. A 10-kilometer run is 6.2 miles, and that sounded like a very long way, longer than I had yet run on my reintroduction to the sport. I knew I wasn't ready for a 10K, but I thought, "Why not? What's the worst that could happen?"

So Sunday morning, I got up early and drove down to Long Beach. The crowd was huge! There must have been 5,000 people jamming the plaza on Shoreline Drive. It almost felt like the crowd at the Formula 1 race earlier that year. I found Mike near the registration table. When I went to register, I discovered it was not a 10K, but a half-marathon! I looked at Mike with incredulity, and said, "A half-marathon? I've never raced that far in my life! What are you trying to do to me?"

He replied, "Well, you don't have to run the whole thing. Just stop when you get tired!" He obviously didn't know me; I knew I wasn't ready for a half-marathon, but I'm a compulsive finisher!

When the gun sounded, Mike and I took off, along with several thousand casual acquaintances. It was really a beautiful morning, cool for November, with a thin overcast. The city of Long Beach was beginning a slow economic recovery since the Navy had left, and some of the more dilapidated buildings were being torn down or renovated. Things felt fresh, as if the whole community was moving forward. We saw spectators lining various parts of the course as we wound our way across the bridge to the Queen Mary, moored alongside a huge parking lot. A loudspeaker had been set up there, and was blaring out the "Rocky" theme as we ran by. At the end of the parking lot was the white dome that housed the Spruce Goose, a fascinating airplane I had been to see several times. On that Sunday morning, the dome was surrounded by five thousand runners strung out along the race course. We came back over the bridge and headed east along Shoreline Drive. Nearing the tall circular hotel at Ocean Avenue, we passed the 5-mile mark, the farthest I'd run in my revitalized life. I was getting tired, but being part of the crowd of runners kept me going. I really was enjoying myself.

Mike, in spite of his solid frame and heavy running style, was still going strong, and I encouraged him to go at his own pace. He nodded and began to accelerate away. By that time we were nearly an hour into the race, and the sun had burned through the haze. The road was beginning to heat up, and consequently, my feet began to get hot. My socks were thin, and I could feel little hot spots where blisters might be forming. I was sweating heavily by that time, and my thick cotton shirt was soaking up a lot of the sweat and dragging against my body. I gradually became aware of a thousand little aches and pains I normally would have ignored. I pressed on—past the 9-mile marker, and then the 10-mile marker. My feet were becoming very sore. By the time I reached the 11-mile marker I was reduced to half-walking, half-jogging, and experiencing a lot of pain. I didn't realize that I hadn't drunk enough water and was dehydrated. I was struggling, but there were only two miles to go; my brain disengaged, and my body took over.

I don't remember finishing, because all conscious thought had receded into the background. All I could think of was the pain and the finish line. I struggled across the line in 2 hours and 20 minutes. My nipples were raw and bleeding, I had blood-filled blisters the size of silver dollars on my feet, and my thighs had rubbed together until there was almost no skin left, but I did finish. It was the kind of mistake I make under the banner of "Anything worth doing is worth overdoing."

I can't even remember if I found Mike, or spoke to him after the race. I was so out of it that I wandered around the parking lot for at least half an hour, trying to remember what my car looked like. I couldn't even remember what color it was. Once everyone else had left, I found it. I drove home very slowly, feeling strangely detached from the world. Everything looked hazy and overcast, even though the sky was still clear and blue. Once I got home, Edna didn't recognize me at first: my skin had turned ashen gray, and my normally blue eyes were almost colorless. The gray was in sharp contrast to the bloodstains on the front of my shirt. In a 'blinding flash of the obvious' I suddenly realized: *It doesn't make sense to always finish everything you start. Some things are unhealthy for you.*

So why had I attempted a half-marathon, when I was not even sure I could run a 10K? There's no logical reason. Logic would have forced me to stop before I hurt myself. But in my heart I'm a runner. I'd been given a second chance, and this time I would not limit myself with preconceived notions of what was possible and what was not. Sooner or later, I would find the limit.

As I began to feel more comfortable with my medication, I trained better and my overall fitness improved. Problems that had hardly been noticeable, like how hard it was to swallow, or button my shirts or tie my shoes, or how I stumbled on familiar words, became noticeable by their absence. I hadn't discussed these minor concerns with my doctor because each one was simply an inconvenience. And I didn't think of tying them all together, since I wasn't concerned with all of them at any one time. It wasn't until I had a name to attach to them that I perceived these individual difficulties as the symptoms of a single process or disease. I was surprised at how putting a name on something offered so much control over it. Now that I knew what I was up against, and had some new ways to deal with it, I could begin to think about all the things I had put off doing. First on that list was to fulfill my longtime goal of climbing Mt. Whitney.

I made the attempt with Tom Dean from work. We had talked about backpacking and camping a few times at work, but we had never considered making a camping trip together. Then one day, out of the blue, Tom asked if I wanted to climb Mt. Whitney over the weekend. We didn't take a lot of time planning the trip, but just threw our camping gear together that Friday around noon, and drove up to Lone Pine. It was about a four-hour drive up to the Owens Valley, so by the time we got the proper permit to enter the wild, it was quite late in the day; we finally started hiking at 4:30, and it quickly turned cool and cloudy. The spot we found to camp that first evening was pretty and tranquil, and probably below the 10,000-foot level. We had hoped to get farther up the trail because we had planned to make a one-day, straight-to-the-top climb from wherever we camped that night. That meant about 9 miles of hiking to climb nearly 5,000 feet to the peak, and then a 3-mile hike to descend at least 2,500 feet to where we could camp that night. On the way up, we would stop only long enough to eat lunch and set up our tent at Trail Camp, at 12,000 feet.

We broke camp on Saturday morning with the sun still below the White Mountains on the eastern side of Owens Valley. The sky was a deep blue-black overhead, with a few stars still visible, but we could just make out a heavy layer of dark clouds moving down from the north. Then for just a few minutes the sun cleared the eastern ridge, and brilliant sunlight fell directly on the eastern face of Mt. Whitney. We were staring at the steepest part of the climb ahead, a broad face of gray granite, covered in a light dusting of snow and ice, with a sharply cut trail zigzagging across it. We were already at 10,000 feet, but the mountain was still a few miles away; I felt intimidated just thinking about the climb of nearly a vertical mile to the top. We hiked the entire day above the tree line on stark, snow-covered rocks and gravel. For a couple of hours we climbed gradually through loose granite to a shelf of bare rock called Trail Camp. From there we could move onto the mountain itself. The original trailblazers who cut the path up Mt. Whitney put exactly 100 switchbacks up the steepest face of the mountain.

Tom was in far better shape than I was, but I stayed with him to the 13,000 foot level. By that time snow had begun to fall. I was miserably cold and nauseous, and thought I might be having a bit of altitude sickness, but I had never had such a feeling before, even when I had flown unpressurized airplanes as high as 16,000 feet. I might have overmedicated myself. I had taken more than my normal dose because I didn't know how much stress such a climb would put on my system. At about 13,200 feet the trail merged with the Pacific Crest Trail briefly, and swung north and then east to conquer the final hump of stone that makes up Mt. Whitney. Only skilled rock climbers attempt to go up the steep eastern face of the peak. Where the trail turned north, the snow deepened, and I knew I was at my limit for the day. I had pushed myself as hard as I could, and I wasn't going to make it to the top. I decided to wait in a sheltered notch in the mountain while Tom went on. Because the weather was getting worse, he didn't waste much time on top, staying just long enough to take a few pictures. I'm glad he did, because those pictures would be a source of delight and inspiration for years to come.

I waited at the notch, well above 13,000 feet, for Tom to return. It was cold but I was out of the wind, and the snow fell quietly around me. It was so quiet I could hear nothing but my own labored breathing. Although I wasn't thinking very clearly at that altitude, I felt strangely patient and composed. I wasn't upset about not making it to the top; in fact, I was actually proud of myself for stopping because it was the right thing to do. Eventually, Tom reappeared out of the snow, and we headed together down the switchbacks to our tent. He had carried a bottle of wine with him to the top, with the expectation that we'd drink it there together. But he brought it back down unopened, and we drank it in the tent that night with the wind howling, and snow piling up against the rainfly. As we warmed our feet and the wine mellowed our mood, Tom said he was very pleased with our day's efforts. He wouldn't let me feel sorry that I hadn't made it to the top. He said, "It's a big mountain, and conditions weren't that easy. Here's the real question: Did you learn what you need to know to make it next time?"

Less than a year later, John Everson, Lewis Prator, Terry Nielsen, Andy Meyer and I came to Lone Pine for a second try. This time we had a plan and stuck to it. We stayed the first night at Whitney Portal, at about 6,700 feet. Next morning we had a terrific breakfast of eggs and hotcakes cooked on a camp stove. Then we packed up the tents, sleeping bags and other trail gear and began to climb. When we got tired, the stronger members of the team, John and Lewis, went back to help the slower members by bringing their packs up to the next stop. We finally set up camp for the night at Trail Camp, where Tom and I had celebrated on our second night out. This time our campsite was a little closer to Consultation Lake, which is fed by melting glacial ice packs from the eastern faces of Mt. Langley and Mt. Whitney. After setting up our tents, and filling our water bottles, we took a break. It was cool, but the sun was still high in the western sky, and there was almost no breeze. Then my buddy John decided to go swimming in Consultation Lake, probably the shortest swim ever recorded! He was in the water and out again in one motion, almost as if he was coming out before he had gotten in, like watching a film clip run in reverse. We were tired, and almost giddy in the thin air, and we laughed so hard we nearly collapsed.

Next morning, the five of us got up, ate a breakfast of instant oatmeal and powdered hot chocolate, packed ourselves some lunch and set off to climb the mountain. Our first challenge was to climb the one hundred switchbacks, then work our way past the notch where I stopped on my first try, and then climb the long traverse of the rounded western slope of the peak. Stage by stage, we worked our way up, and reached the 14,650 foot peak by midday. The sun was brilliant but the air was cold and so transparent that the sky was a deep, deep blue; I swear I could make out a few stars. Andy started acting a little goofy from lack of oxygen, and I thought for a minute we might need to tie him down before he floated away, but he was just enjoying himself. The wind blew fiercely as we huddled in amongst the rocks to keep warm, smiling at each other till our faces hurt. I looked at these four good friends, and rejoiced at the ease of our ascent. Had we not been so short of breath, I would have sung a few bars from the Hallelujah chorus. My heart was certainly singing!

The success of that climb led me to establish an annual backpacking outing with the same group of friends—thirteen in the last fifteen years. Normally, the group consists of Lewis, Andy and Tom from work when they were all in town at the same time, and John Everson, even though John has lived in Virginia for several years. John made our most recent trip after major surgery for a cyst on his spinal cord. I'm afraid we could all see that John was in considerable pain on that trip, and that a lot of his strength had been cut away during the surgery.

Over the years we have hiked many different areas in the Sierras, from Horseshoe Meadow to Tuolumne Meadows on the eastern slope and from Cedar Grove road-end to Wishon Reservoir on the western slope. We normally stayed out three to four days, sometimes making a loop, sometimes just an out and back. Two of the trips that stand out in memory were serious challenges to our strength and backcountry skills. The first was after several years of drought in California. We had been pushing the schedule of our trips forward each year of the drought because we were afraid there might not be enough water late in the season. The year the drought broke we had pushed our trip forward all the way to early June. Then came the March Miracle snowfall - several feet of dense water-laden snow that fell in the last two weeks of March! When Lewis, Andy and I set out from Cedar Grove in Sequoia National Park to walk the 35-mile Rae Lakes loop in early June, there were still several feet of snow at all elevations above 9,000 feet. We rented ice axes and snow shoes and brought plenty of rope and crampons for walking on the icy sections. Each of our packs weighed close to 55 pounds. We even left our cameras in the car in order to save weight, taking along only a small disposable camera. The greatest challenge we faced was the climb over Glenn Pass at 12,000 feet. We were approaching the pass from the east, which meant we would be climbing on deep snow in bright sun. We knew that we should not be on the snow during mid-day because once the sun began to heat the surface we could easily break through the crust and be swallowed up by the deep wet snow underneath. In spite of our best planning, that's exactly what happened. We were probably within 500 feet of the crest when Andy with his small feet and stocky frame plunged through the crust and was nearly lost from sight. Fortunately, we were roped together and there was no possibility that we could actually lose him, but it was considerable work to off-load his pack and hoist it up, and then do the same for him. Once we had him back on solid snow, we put him in the middle of the rope between Lewis and me. I got behind him with the point of my ice axe pointed in his direction and said, "You'd better be prepared to climb as fast as Lewis can or at least faster than me, 'cause you don't want me to catch you." We made that last drive over the top in good shape. We were the first party to successfully cross the pass that year.

The second trip that stands out was a long loop from Tuolumne Meadows, through Glen Aulen, to Miller Lake, over Benson Pass, down into Pate Valley and back up to Glen Aulen and out to the Meadows again. The total was 62 miles and we decided to make it in 6 days. That may sound quite simple, but the elevation ranges from 11,000 feet over Benson Pass to 4,000 feet at the bottom of Pate Valley, and then you've got to climb all the way back up to 10,000 feet to get back to Tuolumne. The route was tough, but what made the trip exhausting was the weather. We walked in rain almost every day, rain so dense that our gore-tex boots were full of water. And it turned cold at times, so cold that we were forced to stop hiking in the middle of the day and pitch our tents then climb in the sleeping bags to recover from hypothermia. Both of those trips were very tough, challenging experiences, but they were made with friends whose skills I respected and whose judgment I trusted.

After my success on Mt. Whitney I knew I could apply the same preparation process to the Long Beach Half-Marathon. My first attempt at that 13.1-mile race had been a foolish mistake. I was unprepared, and should have taken Mike's advice to stop when I got tired. But in the year since, I'd also learned to more accurately gauge my endurance, and regularly went running and hiking to improve my strength. In the fall of 1985, I was certain I could finish a half-marathon, but I also tried to set a realistic time. My goal was to finish in less than two hours. This time the event was even better supported than the first, including water stations every mile, and I was careful to drink water at every opportunity. I was also able to appreciate the fan support and the many bands that lined the streets of downtown Long Beach. I was comfortable throughout most of the race, and just made my target time, getting across the line in 1 hour, 59 minutes. Near the end I had to walk part of the way, so there was still considerable room for improvement.

Throughout the following year, I continued to improve my training schedule, and gradually increased my total mileage. By November of 1986, I had improved to another full level of readiness. I was hoping to run the Long Beach race at 8-minute-per-mile pace, which would have brought me in around 1:45:00. Much to my surprise, the run seemed incredibly easy, and I achieved a breakthrough time of 1:40:08. I'm not sure why I ran so well. Maybe it was a combination of factors, but it took several years to get that kind of time again.

Chapter 4

Learning to Live Well

My improvements did not mean I was gaining the upper hand over the disease, because there is no accurate measure of the disease itself. What is measurable is the ability to manage the symptoms, and perform the daily functions of living. A couple of different scales, based on a series of physical skills, are used to assign grade levels to the patient's condition. One is the Hoehn-Yahr scale, and the other is the UPDRS, or Universal Parkinson's Disease Rating Scale. In my case, the symptoms were minimal when I was properly medicated so I was still regarded as level one on the Hoehn-Yahr scale. I think the reasons for my good fortune were that I normally maintained a high level of fitness and that in young-onset patients PD seems to progress far more slowly than in older patients.

During the mid-1980's, my boss, Tom Dean, had been promoted to manager of Corporate Training and Development, and I got the opportunity to take over Technical Training. Tom and I had worked closely together for several years, and yet I knew surprisingly little about his personal history. I knew he ran, and had tremendous focus, and was compulsive about running every day. When he suggested I run with him while on a business trip, I was afraid I wouldn't be able to keep up, but he willingly adjusted his pace to something I could manage. As we talked about running, it became clear we had reached a similar point in our lives through very different paths. Tom was a product of the running boom in the early 70's. He, like many others, had decided he needed to change his lifestyle after his uncle died suddenly from a heart attack at age 42 while playing tennis. Tom was a high school teacher at the time, barely 30, somewhat overweight, and spent most of his day in the classroom. He was not happy with his self-image, and wanted to get physically fit. Fortunately, being a teacher gave him both some control over his schedule, and access to exercise facilities. His timing was perfect: he decided to get in shape just as the running trend was starting. So he ran.

I've mentioned that I was into competition, well Tom is into achievement. Whatever he chooses to do, you can count on him doing to the fullest. He had never been a serious athlete as a kid, in fact, he had never run a mile before, but as he went from one mile to two, and worked his way up to 4 and 5-mile runs, he gradually became aware of his potential. By the time I worked for him at Honda, Tom was a serious runner. He had run several marathons under 3 hours, and qualified for Boston as interest boomed in the event. I remember he was conscious of diet and training requirements that had never been part of my training when I ran in college. I had never heard of carbohydrate depletion and loading until I noticed that the week before Tom left to run in Boston, he was extremely crabby and hard to work with. But I was impressed by his deep commitment to serious competition.

We came at running from different directions. I'd seen myself as an athlete all my life. I loved the sport for its vitality, its friendships, and its competitiveness. I knew myself as a runner, even though I was being forced to re-learn running from the ground up. Although I never made it to the elite level, I was now trying to enjoy a sport that for twelve years had been taken away from me by the mysterious and cruel intervention of PD.

Tom, on the other hand, was devoted to achievement, and became intensely competitive at an age when, just a few years earlier, most running careers would have been ending. Just as I was becoming more comfortable with running regularly, and beginning to achieve small successes, Tom was abandoning competition because he had achieved his most ambitious targets, including successfully completing an ultra-marathon called the "Western States 100" in 21 hours. He had actually run over the Sierra Nevada Mountains for 100 miles, through the night with a flashlight in hand, across snowfields and on dirt paths, and finished in less than a day. Although he did not start running with the goal of competing in the Olympics or even running a marathon, he had competed in, and completed in excellent time, the toughest organized race in North America! Tom was still committed to running every day; he had just decided not to compete any more. Even when he and I were getting ready to go backpacking, he got up early to go for a run.

I was gradually learning more about PD. I got a lot of help from my brother Jim, who lives in Cincinnati, Ohio, where he's a researcher in biochemistry. He sent me all the current scientific literature on Parkinson's and related diseases. I tried to discuss my growing awareness of PD with my neurologist, but he wasn't interested. He was irritated when I suggested alternatives in my treatment, and seemed less interested in keeping up with the literature than I was. After several years of such frustration, I realized I needed a different doctor, one who would be willing to consider other ideas, even if they did come from the patient. It took a while, but I eventually found the kind of doctor I was looking for through the National Parkinson's Foundation. The NPF sponsors several Centers of Excellence in Parkinson's disease, and one of them was in the neurology center at USC's Keck School of Medicine. That's where I met Dr. Cheryl Waters. In addition to her training in neurology, she is a Movement Disorder Specialist and an expert on the medications used in treating Parkinson's disease. Her expertise in the specific problems facing Parkinson's patients has helped me understand much more about my condition, and has helped prepare me to help others with the disease.

I was fortunate to have a job that I could manage in spite of the PD, and to be in a company that didn't regard me as "handicapped." Once I learned how to use the medications effectively, most of the time people were unaware of my condition. I continued to grow on the job, and was promoted to manager of the Service Training department despite Honda's awareness of my PD. I was able to travel regularly on the job, and established a circle of friends and colleagues in the technical training field and in the automotive business. I tried to stay at my best by living a healthy lifestyle, eating within reason (except for cookies) and trying to keep out of harm's way. I also continued to train diligently, to hike as often as time and weather allowed, and to occasionally ride my bicycle when I felt the need to back off from running.

Running was a solitary pursuit most of the time, but I always enjoyed finding a friend to run with. My first running partner, Mike Carbuto, had moved away within a few months of that first half-marathon, and although he came back to town for certain events, I saw very little of him. For a couple of years I was able to run before work with Gunnar Lindstrom, a fellow manager. Gunnar was a natural athlete, a former world champion motorcyclist, and a good running partner. It helped enormously to share the experience with someone, but before long there was a round of management changes, and Gunnar was reassigned to Honda Research and Development, so it was back to running by myself.

Keeping your training at a high level of commitment can be very difficult when you run alone. But as a military pilot I had learned to maintain an intense focus. To line up your aircraft for a night landing on a pitching carrier deck in rough seas, you have to have perfect vision to clearly see what you're doing. But it may be even more important to have what I call "perfect focus," the ability to not only see things clearly, but also to focus on one thing at a time—to the exclusion of everything else. The result? You see very little outside your own needs. Being blessed (or cursed) with perfect focus means you probably won't see much of the world around you, unless it piques your interest. This may seem like a very selfish worldview to some, but it can keep people alive in difficult circumstances. I think my tendency to focus on what I'm doing has helped me maintain my training habits over the years. It would be easy to lose focus, and lose my mobility with it. I'd already been through a cycle of lost-and-found mobility, and I didn't want to repeat it. I no longer took my mobility for granted—I saw a vivid reminder of what the future might look like each time we visited Edna's parents.

I was always a physical risk-taker. I loved riding my motorcycle, flying, and climbing. I liked being in high places, with my face to the wind. I never saw myself as a daredevil, but I felt a constant need to test myself against my peers, and against my self-image. As a youth I had a great deal of confidence in my physical strength and dexterity. When I was diagnosed with Parkinson's disease, the doctor said I was permanently grounded from flying. He also insisted I give up the motorcycle, and I believed him. I eventually gave up major portions of my normal activities, and with them went portions of my self-respect. I began to feel even simple tasks were imbued with risk, because I was losing confidence in my body. But it hasn't been nearly as bad as the doctors thought it would be. One idea that helped me deal with these new circumstances came from a class I took at work on "customer relations."

The central idea went something like this:

> *Some people treat everything that goes wrong in their lives as a personal tragedy. When bad things happen in society, they have the sense that they are the intended targets of those events. The world, it seems, is against them. From their point of view, they were never given a proper chance to succeed. Others, given similar events, may treat these events as merely obstacles to be overcome. They face the challenge head-on and either beat it or find a way around it. Either way, they emerge victorious. This may not be the result of either greater intelligence or better luck, but rather a positive attitude toward the external world. Events are merely events. The meaning or significance is our own interpretation.*

Is my life a tragedy because I might have been more successful without Parkinson's disease? I have no way of knowing, and besides, I can't turn in the hand I've been dealt, and ask for a new set of cards. Although PD is a genuine inconvenience, I've never felt victimized by it, just forced to live with it and adapt to it. This disease is not my fate or destiny; I am just someone who happens to have Parkinson's disease.

One day a young woman at work asked me, "Do you know why you got Parkinson's disease?" It struck me as an odd question because we had been talking about the disease for several minutes, and I was certain I had mentioned that the cause of PD is still unknown. So how could I know why I got it? It could be internal, an inheritable genetic fault or predisposition, or external, the result of some infection or environmental toxin, or a combination of the two. In my case, I've studied my family history several generations back, and can find no written record of direct ancestors with the disease. I consider it more likely in my case to be the result of some toxic exposure, possibly related to Agent Orange in Vietnam. But looking at the young woman, I could see she wasn't thinking in such terms.

"I know why you got it," she said.

"Why?" I asked.

"You got it because you're going to do something about it."

"That's a very lovely thought," I said. But in the back of my mind I could only ask myself, "Yeah, that sounds great...But what shall I do?"

The question: "Why do bad things happen to good people?" or its more honest corollary, "Why me, Lord?" are really questions that imply a victim mentality. They are not questions that anyone can answer without knowing the mind of God. For me, a more meaningful (though cruder) question would be: "Shit happens... so what am I going to do about it?" My Parkinson's disease is no more than a random event in nature, no matter whether it was triggered by Agent Orange in Vietnam, or the weed killer on my front lawn. I don't believe that God inflicted it specifically on me, either as a character test or as punishment. It just happened. I can deal with it and move on, or I can give up and succumb to it. I prefer the attitude of my fellow Parkinson's sufferer, Jim Wetherell, whose motto (and website address) is "I never give up." Declaring "I will survive" is a huge first step. Once said, it must be followed by meaningful action. Okay, you plan to survive, but how? What you do to survive depends on the tools you've acquired thus far in life - the bigger your toolkit, the better your chances. That toolkit needs to be stuffed full of knowledge and skills and resources. It needs to be overstuffed with friends and family. And it needs to be added to frequently. The skills and knowledge required for survival must be continually updated because they have to work in a continually evolving environment. Today is not a final test; it's just the portal to tomorrow. If I pass this level, I simply get to go to the next one, like a Nintendo game.

Chapter 5

On Shaky Ground

Living in Southern California is boring to some people and risky to others. First there is the lack of seasons, and second, the lack of stability. The earth tends to move from time to time. In October of 1987 a major earthquake hit Whittier. The initial tremor was around 6.1 on the Richter scale, enough energy to cause major structural damage to many of the older buildings in town. Naturally, I was away on a business trip—I've come to realize that the only time things go wrong is when I'm not there to deal with them. This time I happened to be in Las Vegas for a new car introduction. The quake hit on a Thursday morning, and I didn't hear anything about it until late that evening. By the time I got home late Friday, my house was filled with "guests" who had no place to stay because their homes were destroyed. Edna had been home with the kids when the quake hit, but she was upstairs, and the kids were down in the kitchen. By the time she got downstairs, the kids were huddled under the butcher-block table in the middle of the open kitchen, surrounded by fields of broken dishes, packages of food tossed from the cupboards, and the crushed remnants of our liquor cabinet. The kitchen reeked of whisky, amaretto, rum and more, and the kids were stuck in the middle of it, frightened but okay.

That earthquake sent Edna into a panic, and no one operates well in a panic. Her panic was prolonged because the earthquake was not a single event. The big shaker was followed by multiple aftershocks for several days. In fact, we were still calling them aftershocks as much as a year later.[8] Edna says she lost a big bunch of IQ points that morning. Thank goodness she has strong "emotional intelligence" to balance her out. Luckily, my sister Kippi was on her way to work nearby at the time, and came over to help Edna clean up. Eileen (nicknamed Kippi) is a lot like my father: calm in a crisis. Thankfully, she and Edna are quite close, and help each other whenever they can. The upshot of all this? Edna wanted to leave California! And she wasn't alone. In fact nearly 25% of the kids registered in the Whittier School District at the beginning of the school year were gone before the end of the term. But I was committed to my job, and we had just invested in adding on to our house. Tom Rickard, an architect friend from my days at the University of Washington, had designed an 800 square foot addition just a year earlier, and I had done all the finish cabinetry by hand. I didn't want to leave either our home or my job, but I did want to make Edna happy.

The solution? Buy an escape route. We decided to look for a weekend cabin in the mountains, preferably in Big Bear. We made several trips up the mountain to find the right place. On one of those trips David, who was nine at the time, asked, "Why do all the cabins have crazy names like Robin's Roost?"

"Well," I said, "when people invest in a special place like a mountain cabin, they want everyone else to think of it as special too. So they give it a special name." He sat quietly for a minute, and then said, "I think we should name our cabin "Bob"."

Edna and I looked at each other, and kind of nodded.

"Yep, I think you've hit the nail on the head, son. We're looking for "Bob"."

It took a lot of looking, but in March of 1989 we finally found "Bob" in the Moonridge area of Big Bear Lake. It would not have been possible to afford the place without help from Edna's father, Peter, because we always spent nearly all the income we had. We did have enough money for the down payment, but Peter gave us the cash

---

[8] Edna insisted that it was foolish to try to degrade them by calling them aftershocks. To her they were each a fresh earthquake and the panic would rise again.

for the seller, and we drew up a finance agreement, and scheduled the payments to him over the next ten years, just like he was a bank. At the time, Edna was only working part-time in the Whittier library, and finishing her Master's degree in Library Science. It was her second master's degree. Since I hadn't completed the doctoral work I'd started at UCI, she would soon academically outrank me! Fortunately her father had closed out a major investment at the same time we found the cabin we liked and could afford. With his help and cash in our hands, we made an offer and the seller accepted.

The cabin's structure was in excellent condition, unlike our first house in Santa Ana, but the furnishings left a lot to be desired. So I got busy designing and building a complete set of furniture for it. First was a master bedroom suite, with a queen-sized bed, dresser and nightstands all made out of aged walnut. That set, and a hutch I made of birch and alder, are among my best pieces. I recently added three new pieces, a coffee table, ottoman and end table, all of cherry. I hope they'll become family legacies, along with the many beautiful and detailed hand-stitched quilts Edna has sewn over the last few years, some for friends, some for family, and others just for the cabin. I think both Edna and I are more proud of things we've made than anything else, even our academic achievements.

A lot of my self-image has been rooted in the notion of competence. Like my father, I enjoy working with my hands. I feel good about the things I can do like making furniture, or designing a model airplane, or diagnosing car trouble, or even tying my shoes and getting to work on time! But Parkinson's is a progressive disease, and I often wonder how I will regard myself when I cannot do these things anymore. Can I substitute Velcro for shoelaces, and gracefully accept the limits my doctors want to impose? This is not an idle speculation, because I am currently confronting the challenge of keeping my shoes tied. When I'm dyskinetic, my feet rub uncontrollably against each other, and loosen my shoelaces. This dyskinesia happens frequently when I'm eating, so my feet start flopping back and forth, and I drop food on my shirtfront and sleeves. The resulting disheveled look, with the stained shirt and flopping shoelaces, is a dead giveaway that I've just had lunch.

What I see in the mirror is not exactly the image of the former Navy pilot I still see in my head. Where, I wonder, will it go from here?

I've learned that it's important to decide for myself what I can or cannot do. Doctors and friends, with the best of intentions, have advised me not to attempt anything stressful or remotely dangerous. Usually because they don't want to see me injure myself, but sometimes simply because they don't want to have to worry about me. They may genuinely worry about me, and want to protect me, but they cannot judge the importance of certain activities in fulfilling my own psychic needs. Had I the opportunity to turn back the clock to the moment I was diagnosed with PD, I would have fought a lot harder to keep my pilot's medical certificate, and my motorcycle.

Since then, I have learned not to give up on the things that are important to me without a fight. I try to make it my responsibility to decide when, and if, I will reduce my activities. Although I depend almost entirely on my doctor to prescribe appropriate medications, I have to decide how best to use them, because I'm the only one who can feel what my body is doing. I have to be very careful when I drive because one of my medications can make me sleepy in short bursts. If I start feeling drowsy, I get off the road and rest a while. I know my medications lose their effectiveness by late afternoon, so I make sure I arrange my schedule to avoid any heavy physical demands late in the day. I try to have meetings in my building, rather than elsewhere on campus, so I won't be stressed out or cramping up when the meeting starts. I try to minimize the stress in my life, because my PD symptoms increase dramatically under stress. Of course I don't always succeed.

That's why running is so important: it helps me manage stress, and gauge my daily condition. My efforts to stay fit have been critical to my success in managing PD. Taking an active role in understanding the disease process and its treatment has also helped. I often struggled to get my first neurologist to listen to my concerns. And as I researched current treatment ideas, I found he was less informed than I was! I tried to convince him I might benefit from an additional medication called selegilene, its generic name, sold under the trade names Eldepryl and Deprenyl. Selegilene was given to new PD patients in a large-scale trial called the DATATOP study. The result? It seemed to stave off the need for Sinemet for up to a year. I figured that if it slowed the disease process for new patients, it would certainly be worth adding to my regimen. Selegilene belongs to a class of drugs called MonoAmineOxidase (MAO) inhibitors, and was first investigated as an anti-depressant, but later was discovered to slow the loss of dopamine-producing neurons. Once I was able to convince Dr. Beck to prescribe it for me, my performance improved in several areas. I began to work out harder as a result, and my running improved. In the 15 or more years since then many new drugs for Parkinson's have been introduced and I will deal with some of these later in this narrative.

Chapter 6

Running Hard

The key to successful running is to keep everything in balance—whether you have Parkinson's disease or not. For each of us, life is a constant balancing act; we try to keep personal needs, fitness, work, and family activities in the right proportions to ensure our mental and physical health. My balance point is probably different from most, and weighted toward physical health. Running has been especially rewarding when my medications were properly adjusted to my body's needs; I felt like a normal, healthy person, in tune with my body. Occasionally, on long runs when the endorphins kicked-in, I felt like I could cruise forever, in tune with the whole universe. I can recall a couple of those moments of running perfection with such clarity I can almost taste them.

I reached the high point of my second life as a runner in 1990-91. I was 47 years old, and for a while the endorphins kicked in regularly. I got my 5K time under 20 minutes for the first time since college. I dropped my 10 K time under 45:00, and in February of 1991 I cruised to a 1:37:08 in the Lakewood half-marathon. That's 13.1 miles at slightly over a 7-minute pace. What a pleasant surprise! My parents were visiting that weekend, and they had come along to watch the race that morning. I knew I was in good shape, so I told them to be sure to be at the finish line about an hour and forty minutes after the start. All through the middle miles of the race I felt great. For about three of those miles, I even dropped the pace under 7 minutes per mile. I was tiring by the ten-mile mark, but able to hold my pace at about 8 minutes per mile through the final three miles. When my family got to the finish line, I was already there waiting for them with a huge grin on my face. I felt wonderful until the fall.

Around the first of September that year, I borrowed a car from work, and took a trip from L.A. to Seattle with my son David, camping along the way. He was 12 years old, just a couple of months from becoming a teenager. We stopped to see Hearst Castle in San Simeon, and visited the Exploratorium, the science museum in San Francisco. It's a great place for inquisitive young minds because the kids get to touch almost all the exhibits. We drove up the coast, stopped for a walk in the redwoods north of Eureka, and played Frisbee on the beach in Coos Bay, Oregon. While we played, I told David about the meteoric life of Steve Prefontaine, the marvelous Olympic runner who grew up in that small fishing town, and died before he had a chance to fulfill his Olympic dream. From Coos Bay, we pressed on to Tacoma, Washington to spend some time with Tom Rickard, a friend from college days at the University of Washington.

Tom was a little older than I was, and when I met him, he'd already worked a few years as a landscape architect before returning to school for his architectural design degree. A talented artist, Tom included me on his visits to art galleries, taught me the rudiments of drawing and watercolor painting, and introduced me to a group of architects and artists I would never have otherwise met. Tom is recognized as an excellent architect and designer, and has created several impressive houses and large-scale housing complexes, but he prefers to live very simply. He still works for the same small architectural landscape firm he's been with since our college days, and he lives in a tiny suburban house in a middle-class Tacoma neighborhood. The house is jammed from floor to ceiling with books and paintings, both his own watercolor work, and the work of many other artists he's collected. I never figured out why an architect so devoted to Frank Lloyd Wright would choose to live in a rented house in such an uninteresting neighborhood, but that's just one of many things I've never understood about Tom. Over the years, his eccentricities have deepened, and he remains a confirmed bachelor for life.

I remember on the first night of our visit watching the science-fiction movie "Dune" while sitting in a small iron-rimmed hammock-type chair...something straight out of the 1950's. I just couldn't get comfortable, and I squirmed in that chair throughout the movie. The next morning, when I got up early to run around the track at the neighborhood junior high school, I noticed a funny, lumpy feeling in my left buttock. At first I didn't think much about it, but it didn't get any better as I loosened up during the run. After breakfast, David and I drove up to Seattle to visit another old college friend. This one I hadn't seen in a long time, and I was more than a little anxious.

Linda and I had been lovers during my senior year at the University, and we were never sure where the relationship was going after graduation. Every time we got close to saying something meaningful, we'd steer away from it. We both knew I had to honor my commitment to the Navy, but she too had made a commitment, to her parents, that she would finish her degree, and that was a year away. When I left Seattle with my degree and my Navy commission, we parted as lovers, but parted nonetheless. She wanted to finish her degree, and I couldn't argue with that. While I finished my first year of flight training in Pensacola, Florida, she graduated with a degree in French. I asked her to join me in Pensacola, but she decided to stay in Seattle, and complete a master's degree in Library Science. After another year of letters and phone calls, and one brief visit, she had another degree, and I had a set of orders to Sangley Point Naval Air Station in the Philippines. I knew the time had come to make a decision, and I finally asked her to marry me, but by then it was too late. We had drifted too far apart over those two years of separation. As David and I pulled onto I-5 north that morning, I realized that those two years had stretched to more than 23. Linda still worked in the main Seattle Public Library, and I was curious to see how she had changed over the years. She'd been married a little longer than I had, and had a daughter named Cara. I laughed when David asked me if it was all right with Mama for us to meet with my old girlfriend.

I told him, "As long as we just talk, I think it should be okay."

I was a little anxious about the meeting, but I was also suffering from the pain in my lower back. That funny lump had turned into a real pain in the butt. By the time we reached the restaurant where we were to meet Linda that pain was really getting to me. Linda arrived, looking much like I'd expected, still very attractive, with her elegant face framing dark eyes and that mysterious smile. After 23 years we both looked a little older and a bit heavier, of course, but she seemed very comfortable with herself. I, however, was in such pain that all I could think of was to ask her for a couple of aspirin!

As we talked, I could see she was checking David out pretty carefully. After a lull in the conversation she turned to David and said, "You really are quite a handsome young man. Do people say you look more like your father or your mother?"

David lowered his head a little, and looked at her from under his long, dark eyelashes. "Most people say my mom, I guess." He glanced quickly over at me to see what I thought of his answer. Then Linda showed us pictures of her daughter Cara.

I said, "Looks like Cara had the same good fortune to look like her mother." Linda just smiled, and then quickly shifted the conversation to her husband, Steve. He was doing well, she said. He liked his work, and had a lasting interest in Formula 1 car racing. I told her Edna was also a librarian, having completed her degree after the kids were in school, and had almost no interest in cars at all. It was clear Linda didn't want to talk about our old relationship, at least not with my son alongside. The conversation never really got any deeper than that, and after a brief, pleasant visit, David and I drove off to visit the air museum at Boeing Field.

Back in the car, the pain increased so rapidly I couldn't focus on driving, and I couldn't even find Boeing Field, which is nearly two miles wide and four miles long! I told David I was sorry he had to miss the museum, but I had to get back to Tom's in a hurry and lie down. From then on, for the next few days, I was in a haze of pain. I had somehow herniated two discs in my lower back, and both bulges were pressing on the spinal cord and inflaming the sciatic nerve in my left leg. After several trips to the emergency room for X-rays and painkillers, I realized the problem was not improving at all. If anything it was getting worse and I was running out of time on my vacation. Regardless of the pain, I had to get myself, David, and our borrowed car back to L.A.

I drove the 1200-mile return trip with my left leg completely numb below the knee, and in excruciating pain above it. I seriously considered putting David in the driver's seat, but eventually had enough sense to give up the idea. The first night we stopped at a small hotel in Yreka, California. Although it was past Labor Day, and the weather was already turning cold there, the motel had not yet closed the swimming pool. The water temperature was just below 50 degrees. I eased myself into the pool, and hung in that icy water until the lower half of my body was totally numb. What blessed relief! For nearly two hours I felt no pain. But it was only a temporary solution. I don't remember anything about the rest of the drive home. For the next few weeks I was flat on my back. I took heavy doses of aspirin, then stronger anti-inflammatory painkillers, then a packet of steroid pills taken over several days, followed by X-rays and finally an MRI that showed herniated discs at L4 and L5, both with 8mm bulges pressing on the spinal cord. By that time, my neurologist in Whittier was certain I needed surgery to relieve the pressure on the spinal cord. But after my previous experience with surgery, I was more than a little skeptical. Even if I did need the surgery, I wasn't sure he would be the doctor I'd choose to do it.

I went looking for a doctor who might suggest alternatives to surgery. After a couple of months, I found Dr. William Dillin at the Kerlan-Jobe Orthopedic Center. The center was well known because it treated all the major sports teams in Los Angeles, and Dr. Dillin was supposed to be their best back specialist. He was about 5'6" tall, weighed maybe 150 pounds, and seemed to be constantly on the move. He had recently operated on Vlade Divac, the center for the Los Angeles Lakers. I was glad to get in to see him. If I needed back surgery, I wanted it done by the best.

When I handed him the huge packet of medical records I'd accumulated in those 2 ½ months, he barely glanced at the MRI and X-ray films, and then settled in to examine me. After making me sit and stand and try to walk, and nodding several times, he really didn't offer any new ideas or information. Actually, he seemed to be waiting for me to say something that would tip him off as to which way to go.

"Doctor, do you mind if I ask why you barely even looked at those MRIs? They cost my insurance company nearly $1,400."

"I don't operate on pictures. I operate on people."

"But you can see those two big bulges so clearly. They're obviously pressing right on the spinal cord, and causing this pain and all this numb area in my calf and foot."

"What you may not realize is that I could pull ten people your age in off the street and give them all MRIs and maybe seven of the ten would show similar damage, but only one or two might be experiencing pain. The body finds ways to adapt."

"But what about all this numb area in my leg and foot?"

"I don't operate for numbness. My decision to operate or not is really based on your answers to just these two questions. Right now, are you in pain you can't stand?"

"Well, no. I've been living with this pain since September. At least now I can walk to the bathroom rather than crawling on my hands and knees."

"Do you think you're getting stronger or weaker each day?"

"Well, I can do a lot of things better now than a month ago, but look at how much muscle I've lost in my left calf."

"Listen to yourself. You say you can live with this level of pain, and you're getting stronger each day. Every day you can answer those two questions positively, that's another day we won't do surgery. I'm going to recommend aggressive physical therapy"

I finally realized that I'd been trying to convince him I needed surgery, when in fact, I came to see him because I wanted an alternative. Here he was offering me an alternative, and I was trying to talk him out of it. I had to learn when to stop selling!

"Yes," he said, "There are two herniated disks with large bulges pressing on the spinal cord, but the body often finds ways of adjusting. I think you can recover your strength, and overcome this pain faster through physical therapy than you would from the surgery. The long-term prognosis is about the same, with or without surgery."

I'd say Dr. Dillin was probably the most straightforward doctor I had ever met. He just gave you the truth, as he perceived it without any filters. He was definitely not a fan of elective surgery, and I was glad to be working with him. When I told my neurologist in Whittier I'd decided not to go through with the surgery, he got angry with me for not trusting his judgment. That's when I knew it was time to find another doctor, not only for my back problem, but for my PD as well.

Since our return from the trip to Washington, I'd been flat on my back for nearly 2 ½ months. Now I could get around fairly well, and was driving myself to physical therapy sessions four or five days a week, from mid-December until the end of January 1992. After the holiday break, I would stop by the office on my way home from therapy. I couldn't sit through a whole day at the office until nearly the third week of the New Year. My therapy included working out on both a stationary bike and a treadmill, so about the time I returned to work full-time I got right back into running outdoors again. The therapy had not only relieved the back pain; it had improved my overall fitness. I returned to competition by entering the Redondo Beach Super Bowl Sunday 10K race, and ran a 48:09, just two minutes slower than my last 10K before the injury. I was very happy to be back on my feet. Recovery took four months from the time I went down, but I avoided surgery, and my back has been far less troublesome since. My times, however, have never returned to what I was running before I got hurt.

Chapter 7
Building a Team

I joined American Honda in 1975. At that time, automobile service was a small department in a small company. Honda had only been in the automobile business since 1969, and they were only selling one car in America, the Civic. I stayed with Honda while it grew from a motorcycle company into the fourth or fifth largest (depending on how Chrysler was doing on any given day) automotive company in North America. Along the way, many good things have happened, but one of the best for me was the development of the corporate recreation center, and a corporate culture that encourages associates to train and stay fit. We now have a Honda Running Club, a Honda Bicycle Club, racquetball courts and a host of other activities including skiing, photography, and even language studies. Instead of forcing myself to get up early and run alone, I could head over to the rec center at lunchtime, and run with a committed group of friends, then shower and be back at my desk refreshed and ready to tackle the afternoon workload.

I joined the Running Club in 1994, and began to train regularly with other team members. With Running Club backing, I found my training improved, not quite up to my '91 level; but I became a regular competitor for the team, and began to race when I wouldn't have otherwise—I didn't want to let the team down. I turned 50 years old that spring, and I knew my fastest running was in the past, but success isn't always based on faster times. *Racing* may be about fast times and beating your competitors, but *running* has more to do with meeting personal goals and expectations. I thought turning 50 would move me into an easier group of competitors, but of course all my toughest competitors moved with me! Still, I enjoyed trying to win my division at the company 5K, where I first met Mike Delgado.

Mike was making that difficult transition from former racer to recreational runner. He came to Honda from EDS, the computer software company, while Ross Perot was still its CEO. Mike was one of many caught up in the enthusiasm and endless work Perot seemed to generate, but like many EDS employees he was so committed to work, he forgot how to live and have fun. For Mike, submerging himself in that intense environment was easy because he'd been raised in a relatively poor family, and was hungry for success. But when he came to Honda, Mike was looking for a little relief, a chance to breathe on his own time, and "find himself" again. When he came to Honda, he had moved to California, got a place near the beach, and returned to running. While still in transition from the frantic EDS lifestyle to the more deliberate pace at Honda, he ran the 5K at the company picnic. Mike later described the race at a Running Club awards luncheon:

> *"I was new to the company and didn't really know anyone. I was running along, thinking this would be easy. After all, I was still in my mid-thirties, and had already lost a good deal of weight. I'd been a good college runner; I mean I was competitive in the Big-10! Then I see this older guy up in front of me…You know, balding, shoulders kind of hunched a little, and it looked like he was really working hard. So I thought, "I'll go get that guy." He shouldn't be ahead of me this near the end of the race. So I picked it up, but he kicked it down a gear as well, and I couldn't catch him. I was thinking; 'Oh man, have I got some work to do!'"* At that point Michael turned to me and said, "That was you, John, and you beat me!"

Mike Delgado became an important force in the Running Club. As its second president, he inspired lots of enthusiasm for running and walking. His incredibly outgoing personality generated confidence in others. He told them how running had led him out of a marginal life in the toughest part of Detroit, got him into college, and gave him a chance to succeed in the business world. His enthusiasm was contagious -- especially when he talked to kids about the hardships he overcame, and the joy and success running brought to his life!

In 1995, Mike and several other members of the team began to train for the L.A. Marathon. But because of my experience with Mike Carbuto, the Long Beach Half-Marathon was my annual performance check, and I wasn't mentally ready for a full one. Yet in watching Mike prepare himself, and inspire others to prepare, I could see something unexpected happening. Mike wasn't just taking advantage of a pool of dedicated runners. He was cranking people up for the marathon who had never even run before! He was asking people who had never trained for any sport to commit to running and finishing the L.A. Marathon. I thought he was crazy. I wanted to pull him aside and ask, "Haven't you ever heard of Phidippides? He *died* from running the first marathon. You're crazy to think these couch potatoes will ever make it to the finish line. What if somebody really gets hurt? What about the liability?" But I didn't say it out loud, and then, as I began to hear how much progress was being made under Mike's leadership, my thoughts did a U-turn. I began to ask myself, "I wonder if *I* could do it?"

Chapter 8
My First Marathon

In 1996 I finally realized I couldn't put it off any longer. Thanks to Tom Dean, Mike Delgado, and others in sales and marketing, Honda had become the corporate sponsor for the City of Los Angeles Marathon, and I just had to run it. I wasn't alone in the decision. All over the company people were deciding it was time for them as well. Tom Dean was coming out of running retirement, volunteered to take an important job on the marathon committee, and became a prime mover in Honda's preparations for the event. He decided if the company was willing to invest its resources in sponsoring the race, he should contribute some of the expertise he'd gathered in running 25 marathons. He and Mike Delgado didn't know each other well at the time, but as they got better acquainted, they began to appreciate the different strengths each brought to the table. Mike was an enthusiastic spokesperson for the Running Club, and an energetic recruiter. Tom was a very experienced runner, and a seasoned leader in the Honda organization. Together they had a major influence in shaping the event, and promoting it to the community.

Once I had committed myself to it, I told my neurologist, Dr. Cheryl Waters, that I was going to run the marathon. It was not surprising, but she had never had a PD patient run a marathon, so she asked if I would write about my attempt for the National Parkinson Foundation (NPF) newsletter. I thought it was a great idea, and began to keep a journal. Here are some excerpts:

January 30, 1996

Now that my employer has become the sponsor of the L.A. Marathon, I finally made the commitment to run 'the big one.' Lots of changes have occurred in my life since I first thought about running a marathon as a college freshman more than 30 years ago. This is no casual decision for me, because it's all tangled up in childhood dreams that I thought were gone forever. Those dreams have been reawakened. About 60 of my Honda associates from around the world will be competing in L.A.

Since I've never actually run more than 20 miles, even in practice, and that was more than 30 years ago, I have no idea what kind of performance to expect. I really just want to finish. My whole focus for the next few weeks will be on staying healthy, putting in the extra miles, and keeping my commitment to the task at hand. I've even decided to forego skiing until after the race!

Of course, my training regimen has to be regulated according to my medication schedule; I run best in the morning or at noon. Afternoons, when I'm at my low point during the day, are absolutely impossible. I try to run 3 to 5 miles at lunchtime, three times a week, with longer runs on weekends. The best I've done so far is a fifteen-mile training run a week ago. But as I extend the length of my training runs, I've begun to notice pain in my right knee. Injury is a concern for every runner, and probably has nothing to do with PD. The only thing different for me is that if I don't manage my medication properly, I become awkward, and run the risk of falling. It happens occasionally; I just try to bounce up as quickly as I can. Running with PD, as with anything else, is a continuous set of accommodations. It's inconvenient, but I believe I can manage it.

Preparing for a marathon is a challenge for anyone. It requires a huge commitment of time and effort, as well as strategic planning, careful preparation, the ability to adjust to conditions, and the willingness to set a reasonable goal.

Having PD may limit the quality of my performance to less than optimum, but I haven't given up on the idea of success. Success in this case will be to finish the race, at a run or a walk—or to have learned enough through my mistakes to know that with more careful preparation, I can do it next time. One of the lessons learned from my failure on the first attempt to climb Mt. Whitney was that we're unlikely to succeed at everything we try, but the unsuccessful effort is not a failure, if you learn something from it. Seems to me, we're far more likely to regret the ambitions we never tried to fulfill, rather than those we tried to fulfill but couldn't.

February 2, 1996

I was just in Las Vegas for an auto dealer convention, and it happened to be the same weekend as the Las Vegas Marathon. My knee was too sore to run, but I couldn't help noticing all the runners working out the day before the race. As I rode across town in a taxi that morning, I could see runners with their number bibs and "goodie bags." I guess I was thinking out loud, and said something about wishing I could run the event. The cab driver looked at me in the rear view mirror for a minute, and then said, "You look like an otherwise rational human being. Why would anyone in their right mind want to run a marathon?" I answered, "Well, I don't know. Maybe just because I think I can. I've had Parkinson's disease for nearly 20 years, and yet I think that with the right preparation, I might be able to finish. A couple of the guys I train with are running here tomorrow, and they think I can do it." He was silent for a couple of minutes, and then looked up in the mirror again. "That's about the most uplifting thing I've heard in a long time," he said. Then he smiled and said, "This ride's on me." Life is certainly full of surprises!

February 14, 1996 -- Three weeks to go

On February 4, I ran my longest workout to date: 18.6 miles in 3 hours and 12 minutes. My right knee was extremely sore afterward, and a trip to an orthopedic sports doctor confirmed an irritated ligament (ITB), commonly known as 'runner's knee.' I'm taking anti-inflammatory medication, and will begin physical therapy next Monday. The doctor believes I may still be able to complete the marathon. I'm trying to run at least 4 to 6 miles a day, three times a week, and this weekend I'll try for a full 20 miles at a reasonable pace. My plan is to run as far as my knee allows then switch to a fast walk. After this weekend, I'll taper off my workouts to stay fresh for the actual event.

February 20, 1996 -- Two weeks left!

I almost can't believe it, but after a week of taking an anti-inflammatory that made me ravenously hungry and slightly nauseous at the same time, I was able to run the full 22 miles along the Strand, from Hermosa Beach to Marina Del Rey and back. It's by far the longest I've ever run. I couldn't have done it without having my running club support group alongside. They give me the incentive to run, as well as several different paces to choose from. I seem to be running close to 9 minutes per mile. I feel great, and my daughter even said I look younger!

After the 22-mile workout on Saturday, I had some pain in my right knee, so I kept the appointment with the physical therapist. She made me painfully aware of how rigid many of my muscles are. One of the problems with PD is difficulty getting muscles to relax. She could barely move my hamstrings. So I now have a new stretching routine, with seven new exercises, to be done twice a day, along with the stretches I do for the herniated discs in my lower back. Sounds like a lot of work, but I don't plan to give up any mobility or strength without a fight. This territory is defended inch by inch. I learned how easy it is to give in to other people's vision of you when I simply accepted the loss of my pilot's license. PD affects each of us in different ways. I think it's more important to discover what's possible, than to assume what's not.

As for marathon prep, I'm about as ready as I can get. I'll spend these last two weeks going to work as usual, running easily, resting as much as I can, and giving up my insatiable appetite for cookies; in other words, trying to live like every day counted. It's called staying alive, and it's only temporary.

February 29, 1996

Did I say staying alive (and healthy) is a temporary condition? During therapy for my 'runner's knee' my sciatic nerve problem flared up; I'm now trying to get it under control. With only four days until the marathon, I'm nervous because there are still so many obstacles to overcome. I try to deal with them one-at-a-time, but it doesn't take much imagination to let doubt get the upper hand. The very word "marathon" is intimidating—the first guy who ran this distance died shortly afterward. Just like a high stakes poker game, it's easy to fold when your confidence is low. But you sometimes have to ride out a bet, even when your cards look weak. On the brighter side, Dr. Waters sent me a card that said simply; "Yes, you can." In this case, it's enough to know my wife, my son, and a few friends will be waiting at the finish line. I plan to be there.

March 4, 1996 -- The Day After

I've always heard that success tastes sweet, but for a runner it probably tastes more like Gatorade. When I crossed the finish line in downtown L.A., I picked out my wife jammed in among the thousands of cheering fans. I looked her in the eyes and said, "Never again." Now, after a day of recovery I'm not so sure. My fellow runners tell me that's because the body doesn't remember pain. I do know it'll be a long time before I forget how exhausted I was and yet how good it felt to complete my first marathon!

For someone with PD, the start of the L.A. Marathon could not have been more poignant. The guest of honor on the starter's platform was fellow Parkinson's sufferer, Muhammad Ali. As I jogged to the starting line, I was moved almost to tears to see this magnificent athlete trapped inside his near motionless body. The runners chanted, "Ali—Ali— Ali" as we passed, and I could see his eyes. The warmth of his respect for us as runners inspired me to throw my arms up in uncharacteristic exultation. Characteristic of the day, the local TV broadcast actually recorded my gesture!

Throughout the first three miles I was surprised at the people running beside me: every variety in the catalog of human beings, and all attempting to run a marathon. I was just one among 20,000 out for a 26.2-mile Sunday run! As a kid, I would never have believed it possible.

Miles 5 through 13 were right on schedule, except for a brief stop at mile 8 to tighten my shoelaces, and take my mid-morning medication.[9] Honda hosted the crucial thirteenth mile water station and the cheering of my friends from work helped me prepare mentally for the rest of the run. At the half-marathon mark I was on pace at 1 hour, 58 minutes. I thought, "I've already equaled the longest race of my life, and yet I'm only half done! Now I've got to do it all again." The enthusiasm of the crowd and my natural love of hills caused me to pick up my pace on the next few miles, and around mile 18 I caught my old friend, Mike Carbuto, who had "tricked" me into that first half-marathon. What an incredible feeling, to give him a smile and a nod as I passed alongside, then power on by him, and never look back.

I cruised through the neighborhoods into Hollywood, and hit the 20-mile mark nearly 2 minutes ahead of my 3-hour target. Then the course got tough. Miles 21 through 23 were a drudge, and about halfway through mile 23 my knee had suffered too much downhill strain. The dull ache in my ITB went from a murmur to a scream. No confusion about what it was telling me. I had to walk the rest of mile 23 and most of mile 24. I gave up all the time I had gained, and lost

---

[9] At that time I was taking Sinemet, Eldepryl, and I had added Permax to my treatment. Permax is a dopamine agonist, which helps balance the neurotransmitters slowing down the re-uptake of dopamine.

the remaining cushion between the nine-minute pace and the 4-hour mark. I was discouraged, and sore, but still felt I would finish.

At mile 25, I was prepared to just trudge on in. But the clock showed 3 hours, 50 minutes, still a chance to break four hours! That would require an 8-minute mile pace, and though I didn't think I could do, at least I could try. I came close to stopping a couple of times from pain and fatigue, but in the last quarter-mile my favorite Running Club partner, Aaron Yanagi, caught me and shook me out of the doldrums. We finished together, barely half a minute over the four-hour mark. Mike Delgado, although he'd finished much earlier, was there at the finish line greeting and hugging every team member as they came across.[10]

Stiff and sore, sitting at my desk at work, I've gotten very little done today, but I'm surrounded by people who seem genuinely proud of my accomplishment. What would life be like if every day could be like this? Edna, David and Sarah are thrilled. Even my mother called to congratulate me! And my neurologist is extremely proud. My kids have spotted me three times in the tape from the local TV broadcast. All in all, it's a fabulous day even though it's pouring rain outside— I couldn't care less. Thanks to all of you who made this possible. And special thanks to Tom Dean and Mike Delgado for helping to make my dream a reality.

Later on, I wrote this poem for my associates who spent their Sunday handing out water and encouragement at the halfway point in the race. I wanted them to know how much it helped to hear them cheering every time a Honda Running Club uniform came into view.

---

[10] Mike Delgado finished 86th overall. Tom Dean finished 7th in his age group, which is the same over-50 group I'm in. I finished 122nd in the group.

Water Station: Mile Thirteen

Among the many volunteers
My former boss runs beside me,
Hoping I will take the drink
He offers up.
I take the cup
And drink it gladly.
His face opens in a grin.
We are both pleased.
There are hundreds of you
Who have chosen to work today,
Standing for hours in the Sunday sun
To hand out water to the thirsty thousands.
I just finished my longest race,
And yet I'm only half way to my goal.
Your shouts and smiles bring courage;
Your faces glow with possibility.
I stare at the road in front of my feet.
The path ahead is new and unknown,
Yet equal to the road behind—
Equidistant between the past and future.
Entering this new world,
I choose a faster pace,
For suddenly I am eager
To see what lies ahead.
2/17/97

Although it had to be edited to fit the newsletter, the NPF printed my journal. I received several heartwarming calls and letters as a result. Later I got a call from a former stockbroker in New York who had given up skiing because of PD, but after reading the article he decided to give it another try. He said it brought a lot of joy back into his life. Another call came from a runner in Florida who just wanted to talk about running with someone who would understand what it meant to run with PD.

Chapter 9
Returning to the Air

Publishing my journal entries also got the attention of the local NPF chapter. I met Kim Seidmann, who among her other assignments as West Coast Director for NPF was responsible for organizing a 5K run, part of a series of fund-raising events across the country. The events were to be in honor of Gene Fair, who had young-onset Parkinson's. For some time after his initial diagnosis, Gene had let himself disintegrate both emotionally and physically. Fortunately, his four-year-old daughter stirred him up enough to get out of the wheelchair he'd been in for a couple of years, and get back on his feet again. Soon he started running and competing in 5k's, and became an inspiration to many others. I volunteered to be the local "race director" even though I had no idea what a race director was supposed to do. At least I knew what a good 5k looked liked from the runner's point of view!

Kim and I and several other volunteers worked hard to put on a successful event in Griffith Park. Although sparsely attended by elite racers, as would be expected for a first time event, the race still raised a significant amount of money. In reality, the money we raised had little to do with the event we held, and we assumed that the Parkinson's cause and elite-level road running was not a "logical" match. Later we re-examined that assumption and decided that major running events and Parkinson's awareness could work together *because* it juxtaposes two antagonistic notions: a movement disorder takes on the marathon! We also learned that putting on a good road race takes lots of time, lots of people, and lots of advertising.

Another result of publishing the journal entries was my introduction to the community of PD support groups. A few months after running the marathon, I was asked to speak at a Parkinson's support group monthly meeting in a church in Little Tokyo. I'd never attended a support group, so I was curious but also repelled. Consciously or unconsciously, I had always avoided support groups because I didn't like seeing others suffer. Perhaps I was actually afraid of attending, even though I would be the guest speaker—someone supposedly living well with PD—because I felt like I'd be admitting I was having trouble coping with the disease. In retrospect, I wonder why I felt it was so important to go it alone, insisting to myself that I didn't need the support and empathy of others with PD.

As I prepared my thoughts for the group, I tried to create a positive presentation that focused on how I compensated for PD, and how I managed my medications to get the most out of them. I asked my wife to proofread and edit what I'd written since she had worked as a professional proofreader and was a terrific editor. When she'd finished, I could see she was displeased.

She said, "Well, it's a nice story you tell here, and you tell it well, but where are *we*? What about the rest of us? You sound like you're the only one affected by your disease."

Her question shook me to my very core. I was suddenly staring into a world that had been invisible to me all those years. Was it my pilot-syndrome—my ability to see precisely, but only what directly affected me? I seemed incapable of seeing much beyond myself. Until that moment, I had somehow believed I was handling Parkinson's all by myself. It was another "blinding flash of the obvious."[11] What had been obvious to everyone else was suddenly revealed to me. I genuinely felt as if I had been blind, and now could see.

All those years I had felt in control of things. Since I maintained my job, and could still pursue my interests outside of work, I

---

[11] By this time in my life it had happened so often, that I simply called it another "BFO": that sudden enlightenment around a fact that everyone else has already had to deal with.

thought the impact of PD on my family and friends was minimal. I was wrong, of course. It has always had an impact, both good and bad, on many people around me, though I was mostly unaware of it. When I succeeded, others were encouraged to try a little harder. When I failed, I was not the only one who got discouraged. I learned quite late in life that no matter how well we think we're handling our individual challenges, none of us is really flying solo. This is a family disease, and often a community disease. It touches everyone around you. I did give that presentation to the support group, pretty much as I had originally written it, but then I gave them the second half of the story. I set aside my notes and talked to them from the heart about how badly I misjudged my handling of the disease. That took me into some new and dangerous emotional territory, but I could look at my wife through the tears and see her clearly, perhaps for the first time.

I was visiting Dr. Waters' office three or four times a year to check my progress. She was always very busy, specializing in clinical testing of new anti-Parkinson's drugs. We seldom got much time to talk, but when we did, she listened carefully for things that were important to me. It was her ability to find what was really important to me that brought me back to flying. Because she could see how much it meant to me, she went to bat for me with the FAA. She wrote a strongly worded letter to the Flight Medical Center in Oklahoma, detailing my condition, and asking for my re-instatement to flight status. Because of her recommendation, and her credibility as one of the top Parkinson's specialists in the country, my medical certificate was re-instated. After being officially grounded for ten years, I was finally an aviator once more. What joy that brought back to my life!

My first reaction was to drive over to the local airport a few miles from home, and look up the company I flew for as an instructor while attending Cal State L.A. But the company was no longer in business. So I found a new Fixed Base Operator, and got checked out in a Katana, a new aircraft with a lovely composite body that looks like a high-performance glider with its wings clipped. It's so aerodynamically clean it needs just an 82 horsepower Rotax engine. It took me just two flights to get re-qualified, and I began taking friends along on some flights. I even toyed with the idea of re-certifying as an instructor. But after the initial thrill, I began to realize that much had changed in the flying world, and in my situation. Flying was a lot more expensive, and the air was far more crowded. And when it came right down to it, I probably wasn't as good a pilot as I had been earlier.

One thing that hadn't changed was Edna's discomfort in small airplanes. She was really no more interested in flying in small planes now than she had been 15 years earlier, so after the initial high of being back in the air, I found it became less and less important to me. Just boring holes in the sky got sort of ...boring. And without Edna along I had no interest in flying solo on sightseeing trips.

I thought I might continue flying, if only a few times a year, if I had a couple of flying buddies, so I encouraged my friend Ken to get his license, which he did. But he ran into the same roadblock at home: Sandy didn't like to fly either. So after a few months of fewer and fewer flights, Ken and I sat down at the flight planning table on a Sunday afternoon and opened up to each other.

I said, "You know, Ken, this really isn't as much fun as it should be. I've discovered it's a lot more difficult to keep track of things in the air when you're 50 than when you're 25. And for me to really stay proficient, it's going to take a lot more hours than I can afford. Besides, I'm actually older now than those guys I used to think were too old to fly in Viet Nam and the Philippines. Commander Bush used to fall asleep at the controls and he was only 46! I've got five years on him already."

"I understand, John. And without Edna and Sandy where the hell can we go? There are only so many lunches and apple pie trips I can handle. Even worse, there are just too many planes and too much controlled airspace in this L.A. basin!" We both knew - but didn't feel like admitting – our flying days were numbered. That overwhelming need to be in the pilot's seat had slowly faded away.

I still love flight, but now I have almost as much fun flying my remote control gliders as I do being in the air by myself. From a windy hilltop, I enjoy watching a glider in the magic of flight, guiding it into invisible air currents where it rises and falls like a bird. I enjoy it even more when the glider is my own design.

Dr. Waters had never used the words "you shouldn't," or "you can't." But that didn't mean I had *carte blanche* to do anything I wanted. I'm well aware time moves in only one direction, and I'm getting older like everybody else. She did occasionally remind me that PD is a progressive disease, and my future is not yet predictable.

"Yes," she said, "you are doing very well right now…far better than anyone else in my experience, but neither of us can accurately predict the future. We can't be sure you'll always be like this."

Although I can accept this intellectually, I still resist planning my future around the worst-case scenario. Everyone who is blessed, or cursed, with a competitive spirit eventually comes to a crucial point in life when they can no longer meet the same expectations they did a decade ago, or even a year ago. They're forced to set new priorities: how much to train, how hard to work, how much time to set aside to reach a certain goal. As always, it's a series of compromises. How hard can I push before I get hurt? How much time can I take away from my family responsibilities? But these choices are no different because of PD. Life continually forces us to make choices, to compromise on *this* in order to achieve *that*. As we age we all face a recurring challenge: to learn how to set reasonable limits, without forfeiting or compromising our remaining potential. I think of it as balance- the high wire act of life – and for me, the higher the better!

Achieving balance may require endless maneuvering, but may also prove impossible without major readjustments. Take this book, for example. I worked on it in one form or another for several years, and yet I'm still not sure if it has an audience—I can't say if anyone is impatiently waiting to hear my story, yet I feel compelled to write it. Maybe it's just therapy for my own heart and soul. It's not meant to be my *life's* story—my life is still a work-in-progress, and I hope I'm just getting to the good parts. But this book needs a purpose, and a focus; I want it to carry one message clearly: we must take action to control our own destinies.

For years I used to think: "Any day now I expect to learn what I'm here for." I may never have defined my target clearly, but I think I've discovered what lies at the center of the bull's-eye. It's a modification of a Boy Scout rule I learned as a teenager, but it's taken me a lifetime to simplify it. *I want to leave the world a better place than I found it.* I don't expect to make a big impact, since I'm certainly not among the wealthy or powerful, and it's too late in the game for me to do something dramatic like finding the cure for cancer—or Parkinson's disease. I'm no one's real-life hero. My wife has lived through so many of my mistakes I think of *her* as heroic for staying with me! I don't really know how my kids see me—as their father, of course, but not as a hero. I certainly wasn't a distinguished Navy officer. In fact, to my peers, I was the opposite—a good pilot, but one who wouldn't follow orders or sacrifice himself for the mission, or for the Navy.

I never achieved great success as a runner in high school or college. I did do well in a few races that were important to me, but was never regarded as a lead runner even on my own teams. In the world of competitive athletes, a 4-hour marathon simply qualifies you as a runner, not a heroic athlete.

At work I became a middle manager, leading a department but not a division. I tried to achieve something useful for the company and the technicians we served, instead of reaching for promotions beyond my area of expertise. But I would like to have people remember me as someone who "tried to do what's right," whether cleaning campsites of the trash others left behind, or adding value to the world through my work, my ideas, or my family. Posterity will decide. I hope my children will be able to say I left the world a little better than I found it.

Chapter 10
Getting to Know My Enemy

For several years I felt I was handling my PD successfully. I didn't live in fear of the future, perhaps because I'm not a sensitive or fearful person. If I were, I would never have made it through Navy flight training, or been willing to fly in dangerous conditions. I believed I was responsible for judging the balance between risk and reward. I didn't bother to consult others, or even consider the effect of my decisions on them. If I chose to hike the high Sierras with a heavy pack, I took my chances in the wilderness because the reward—the beauty of the mountains—was worth the risk. I didn't stop to consider the anxiety others might feel, watching me trying to adjust my medications while teetering on the edge of a cliff! I was insensitive to their feelings and fears, because for most of my life I've been just as insensitive to my own. My habit was to plunge in, like my friend John Everson, no matter how cold or deep the water.

Looking back, I know my family must have worried at times. How long would I be able to continue working? What about college plans for the kids? Would there be enough financial support if I were disabled? My introverted, egocentric nature just blanked these questions out of my mind. As long as things were stable, why worry about other possibilities? But of course the fears were justified. I could see how Edna's family had to deal with her mother's PD. Their primary concern, day in and day out, was to care for her, and keep her from hurting herself, by doing for her the things she could no longer manage. Chana never complained about her pain or lack of mobility, but all of us around her were saddened by it. One of the cruelest aspects of Parkinson's is the suffering it inflicts on those who love and care for the person living with the disease; the caregivers may struggle with grief, or a sense of helplessness or loss even more than the persons they're caring for.

My children, David and Sarah were born years after my Parkinson's symptoms had begun, but before I was actually diagnosed. They have no memory of what I was like before PD— they've never seen me without some symptoms of the disease. They probably don't look at me and think about dyskinesia or dystonia, they just think: "Dad's real twitchy today...but that's just the way he is sometimes." They're bright and capable, and a joy to be around. They are, along with Edna, the most important people in my life, and yet I seldom tell them so.

David has graduated from San Francisco State. As I write this, he's working in an audio post-production company, doing sound tracks for television and movies. Earlier he was at Cal State Fullerton, and played trumpet in a ska band. When the band, called "Low Pressure," recorded their first CD, they had a release party at the Whiskey-a-go-go on Sunset Boulevard. They packed the place with their fans and friends. What a thrill that was for Edna and me, to watch our son perform with his band on a professional stage, with teenage girls shouting his name and throwing him kisses! The band worked hard to please their fans, and by the end of the performance, my nice black wool suit David had borrowed was soaked from collar to cuff. I told him, "You can keep the suit. Just make sure you get it cleaned before you wear it to a job interview!"

Sarah is the artist in the family. She's been interested in drama since grade school, and took part in many Whittier Children's Theater productions from about 12 years old until she entered high school. She auditioned and was accepted into the Theater Arts department of the Los Angeles County High School for the Arts. She graduated from there, and auditioned for several college and conservatory theater programs, but wasn't accepted because she'd let her academic grades slide while pursuing her theater ambitions. After high school, she became a puppeteer with the Bob Baker Marionettes, and then moved on to the San Francisco Art Institute where she's now finishing up her fine arts degree. She's into performance art, and is not yet certain how she'll live on that degree, since there are no jobs ready-made for performance artists. But she's a smart, hard-working young woman, who's committed to her ideals, so I'm sure she'll find her way into something meaningful.

David, now 25 and Sarah, 23, know in a deep and personal way that I'm not the only one in the family who suffers from PD. No, I'm not talking about Edna's mother, even though she suffered much more with PD than I have—her battles are now passed. I'm talking about my wife and children. *They suffer with me, and triumph with me.* PD causes a certain amount of tension for all of us. And much more for Edna when she had to care for her mother, and also care about me. I hope she doesn't feel she's my caregiver yet, because, although we both make adjustments to accommodate my Parkinson's, I don't feel dependent on her for help with the normal tasks of daily living. I do depend on her for the kind of help and support given by a loving wife and partner, but not yet as a caregiver. I'm thankful she's better equipped than most to deal with the demands ahead.

No matter how much I love my family, I sometimes put myself at risk just to show the world I'm still in control . . . even if I'm not. I don't want to be drawn into the Parkinson's trap, baited with temptations to "give up." When the doctor tells a patient, "You have Parkinson's disease. It's degenerative, and there is no cure," it would be easy to give up control to the doctor, or to family members, or to emptiness, anger, or despair. I don't think that's in anyone's best interest.

I gave up big parts of my lifestyle at first—flying, motorcycling, car racing—and have grudgingly given up other key activities since, but I fought hard to keep the important things alive—my job and my family. I was fortunate to be able to keep working for nearly 20 years after my diagnosis. I had lots of responsibilities, but was surrounded by talented people who were, and still are, proud of the products they create. I'm thankful the company was more interested in my capabilities than my limitations. They let me create a meaningful career, where I could contribute my best in my area of expertise. Yet they were also sensitive to my needs, and willing to adjust my responsibilities when the workload got too demanding.

Not everyone at Honda has been so fortunate. In 1993 one of my associates was diagnosed with Parkinson's disease. Steve was a lead designer at Honda Research of America. He led a team of designers and draftsmen responsible for creating automobile variations tailored specifically for the North American market. During his early 50's he began to lose control over the movements of his body. As the symptoms grew worse, he became depressed. His wife kept telling him his problems were all in his head, and in at least one sense, she was right. Steve suffered as much from the depression as from the physical difficulties, and was eventually hospitalized in a psychiatric ward. There he was treated for several weeks with Thorazine, but he failed to respond as expected. After a thorough re-examination, the diagnosis was changed to Parkinson's disease.

When Steve first told me his story, I was angry with the doctors who knew so little about PD that they mistook it for psychosis. But the doctors were not alone; Steve's wife was so certain he was losing his mind that she left him, and soon filed for divorce. Over the course of a year, Steve and I talked several times about his situation. I recommended he switch to a doctor more focused on movement disorders, and offered to set him up with the doctors at the USC Medical Center where I saw Dr. Waters. It took him a while to realize there might be better treatment available, so by the time he was examined at the Medical Center, his condition had degraded considerably. At work, he could barely walk from his office to the lunchroom, and when he did make the trip, it was agonizingly slow. His awkward stride made him look like a cartoon character out of R. Crumb's "Keep on Truckin." Lately I've had days when I walk like that myself. Now I know what he must have felt like, unable to control his movements unless he exaggerated them. It's not only awkward looking; it's difficult and painful.

Steve didn't manage his medications well, and occasionally talked about the bizarre hallucinations he was having. I began to realize his experience with Parkinson's disease was very different from mine. His senior management eventually became convinced that he could no longer supervise his design team, and within a year of his diagnosis, he left Honda on full disability. A few weeks later, he called and said he was moving to Colorado. He wasn't in bad shape financially, and had found a nice place near Golden where he planned to live. He also mentioned the new Porsche he'd just bought. I thought that was an awfully fast car for someone in such physical distress, but I didn't want to sound negative, or discourage him any more than necessary. He seemed to have reached a point where he no longer cared whether he lived or not. Perhaps the Porsche was a way to hasten the eventual outcome.

I called him several times during his first few months in Colorado, but each time we talked his conversation was less and less rational. In the middle of an ordinary discussion of the weather in Golden, he would begin to describe the monsters that occasionally surrounded his house when it snowed. At first I thought he was being metaphorical, but eventually I realized he was talking about real monsters; gargoyle-like beasts that looked in his windows, and shouted things at him, and occasionally prodded him toward suicide. Much to my embarrassment, I reached the point where I no longer had the courage to call him, because I was afraid of what I would hear.

I can see now that for many years I had avoided associations with other Parkinson's patients. I didn't feel a need for support groups, and I got very uncomfortable when I saw the challenges other PD patients faced, especially my mother-in-law. I felt a great deal of empathy for her, but didn't picture myself ever facing the same conditions. For a few months after my first marathon, I guess I thought of myself as a minor celebrity in the Parkinson's community, and thought I had something important to share with them. But I soon learned each experience is unique. What works for me may have limited value to someone else—it would be a mistake to generalize from my experience any set of rules on how to deal with PD.

Comparing my experience with Steve's, for example, makes me appreciate the support of my family more than ever. Sarah, David and Edna encourage and help me even when I'm self-centered or grumpy. They always seem to be there when I need them. Nothing is perfect, of course. At times, I felt my needs were *not* being met, and I'm sure at times they've needed more from me. Sometimes I find myself asking questions to the void, "What if I didn't have PD? Would my life be different?" Of course it would, but the questions are irrelevant. My neck gets sore when I spend too much time looking back over my shoulder—I prefer to look ahead!

Once in a while I'll ask myself, "Is it worth all the effort it takes to sustain my career and level of fitness? Why do I push myself so hard all the time? Can't I just relax and enjoy life a little?" My neurologist thinks I'm overextended, and I've realized lately that I'm not doing as well as before, but that's no different for me than it would be for anyone else eligible for the senior citizen's discount. None of us is immortal. We do what works until we can't do it anymore, then we find something else that'll work for a while. We accommodate, and move on.

Once I'd recovered from running my first marathon in 1996, I knew I had to do it again. To the club-level runner, the four-hour mark is the dividing line between the occasional runner and a 'real' marathon runner. My time was 4 hours, and 29 seconds which placed me 3,144 out of about 21,000, even though I was nearly two hours behind the winners. Since the elite runners had finished in almost half the time it took me, I felt quite slow, but Edna reminded me there were still nearly 17,000 people out on the course behind me. I'd come so close to running under 4 hours on my first try that I did everything I could to break through that barrier in 1997.

I began training at longer distances in October, instead of waiting until December. In January I lowered my half-marathon time to 1 hour, 47 minutes, a full ten minutes slower than my personal best, but it was the fastest I had run in nearly four years. I continued to train with my Running Club partners at the beach on Saturday mornings, and moved the distance up from 12 miles to 15, and finally to 19 before the race. I knew I was ready to run. I had a really good base, including two "century" bicycle rides for cross-training, and I had a pacesetter. Tom Dean offered to help anyone wanting to break that four-hour barrier. If we would stick with Tom, he would get us through it.

The evening before the race my wife and I took a room in the Bonaventure Hotel, as we had the year before, and had a pasta dinner with the Running Club that evening. Next morning we joined an inspiring little gathering of Honda runners before the race started. The Running Club had become a team. We had focus, and we knew what our target was. We grouped around Tom, and when the gun sounded we all took off: Tom, Alan Shindo, Dan Louie, Mike Bach, Mark Ziobro, and me.

Mark was one of Mike Delgado's recruits. In his early thirties, and healthy, but inexperienced, this was his first marathon, and just his second footrace. He had no idea what time he could run, but had decided to try to keep up with Tom. Alan and I, second year marathoners, had both just missed the four-hour mark on the first try. Dan Louie and Mike Bach each had a bit more experience, and Mike had run a sub-four-hour marathon in Las Vegas just a month earlier. Tom Dean, of course, had many years of experience; we knew he would keep us on the right pace.

The day was hotter than predicted, and I sweat profusely because of PD, so by the end of mile 4 there was a steady stream of fluid running off the bill of my cap. I knew it would be easy to get dehydrated. From the fifth mile on I forced myself to walk through the water stations because I find it hard to swallow while running, and I had to make sure I drank enough. That made it tough to stay with the group, and put me on the ragged edge of making my target time. I also had to stop around mile 8 to take my morning medications. After each water station I pushed myself to catch up to the group. By the halfway mark, I knew I couldn't stay with Tom much longer.

Alan was the first to drop off the pace, between mile 13 and 14, and I began dropping back just a mile later. After I'd walked through the water station at mile 15, the group was out of sight. Four of the six that started with Tom were still with him. Even though I was off the pace and my teammates were out of sight, it was too soon to give up. At each mile marker I began recalculating the pace I'd have to run to catch up.

During mile 18, I got a small boost by remembering how I'd passed Mike Carbuto during that long uphill the year before. Then at mile 19, I caught and passed one of the Honda runners from the factory in Marysville, Ohio. I began to feel better, but I knew the toughest part of the course lay ahead. At 20 miles, I started calculating how many seconds I could walk each mile to have any hope of breaking four hours. At mile 21, I could afford a 50-second walk. At 23, I had to cut it back to 40 seconds. I knew that for the first time in my life, I was using everything I had, and would hold nothing in reserve.

By the end of 25 miles I was at my limit, but still running. I pushed my legs to give just a little more, willing myself forward. When I finally came around the last corner and saw the big digital finish-line clock ticking from 3:58 to 3:59, I dug deep inside myself, as deep as I have ever gone for that final push...but there was nothing left. The account was empty. No deposit, no return. I felt hopeless but kept moving forward. There was no finishing sprint, I just put one foot in front of the other until I slithered across the line. I stopped my watch at 3:59:10. Fifty seconds to spare! I gave it everything I had. I'm just glad I had no injuries. Edna pushed her way through to the street, and hugged me and held me up. Without her help, I would have fallen down and been unable to get up. In the after-race photo with my finisher's medal, she's there behind me, propping me up like a puppeteer.

All but Alan in our original group had finished under four hours. Dan Louie was just a minute ahead of me at 3:58. Mike Bach was in at 3:54. And Tom Dean and Mark Ziobro had finished together at 3:48. Sometime after I dropped back, they'd looked at each other, and decided to kick it on in—hard. Alan Shindo was not too far behind me, just two minutes off the pace. My finish position was 2,771, so I'd picked up nearly 400 positions by improving my time less than a minute and a half.

I had never felt better in my life. Yet at the same time, I'd never felt worse. I was ecstatic to have reached my goal, but I was also physically and mentally exhausted. And since my Achilles' tendon was sore, I just let everything go for a while.

Chapter 11

The Silent Partner

After the marathon, I kicked back and let things wind down, though not for physical as much as mental and emotional reasons. By spending so much time worrying about the race, I'd dug myself into a hole at work. Afterwards I couldn't focus on either my job or my running. I stopped caring about training, and quickly put on ten pounds. My running mileage dropped well below the level I needed to stay fit. I just decided I'd done enough.

Like a smooth flowing river, Edna and I had shared a comfortable life up to that point, in spite of my PD, and the care she devoted to her parents. We'd floated along in a comfortable relationship, our love founded on mutual respect, and buoyed up by Edna's caring nature. We focused on raising our children to be good citizens, and surrounded them with the affection of friends and relatives. Sound too good to be true? On the surface it was true, but there were also undercurrents in the depths of the river, swirling around submerged, decayed trees with limbs that stretched up toward the surface like the outstretched arms of former lovers. Over time, the riverbanks turned to mud, and the river got dark and cloudy. The water seemed to turn back on itself, the current mysteriously ceased. I found my life was stagnant.

I knew what I should be doing, but just didn't feel like doing it anymore. Was I just bored? Had I failed to fulfill my vision of an integrated intellectual and technical life? Had I slipped out of the mainstream into some tepid backwater because I had grown too cautious? I began to feel an uncomfortable restlessness. My work group was stuck in a small eddy, endlessly twisting around the same issues. Had I spent so much energy on the marathon that I was neglecting them and my responsibilities? I was supposed to be a manager and leader of my department, but I couldn't seem to jolt them free. The constant drive to move ahead was gradually being replaced by an effort to simply maintain coherence in the work we did. My vision for technical training no longer generated any unity or enthusiasm in the department, or in the training centers where our work was put to the test. I suppose I could have dismissed the whole thing as part of a typical mid-life crisis, but I had the uneasy feeling it was somehow tied to my Parkinson's disease.

I tried to stay fit by riding my bicycle, but a bike is a lot more awkward to haul around than a pair of shorts and running shoes so I did it far less often. I only rode on Tuesday evenings with some guys from work who got together on the bike path at Redondo Beach. We usually rode about 20 miles, although toward the end of summer, I rode on Saturdays as well, and managed to push the mileage up to prepare for the Amtrak Century. The "Amtrak" is a really nice 100-mile bike ride from the Irvine train station to the big depot in downtown San Diego, with a return ride on the train. I rode well on that ride, finishing in about 6 and ½ hours, among the first one hundred of the 800 participants. I even got a great photo of myself on my new Cannondale bike. I happened to see the event photographer setting up as we reached the first rest stop, so I gave him a smile, and tried to look like I was enjoying myself. All in all, I was pleased with my effort, but it was just a small bump on a long downhill slide.

The rest of my life was a mess. I was struggling unsuccessfully to maintain control of the department. The staff was suffering, and I was feeling the stress. I had let things get out of control, and my management was losing confidence in me as a result. I could see there was a problem, but I couldn't identify the cause. I was wondering why everyone had turned against me after years of success. My boss made it clear I was in deep trouble, and gave me an unsatisfactory performance review. He said I'd lost my "edge." I honestly didn't know what he was talking about, because I couldn't see it. I did have enough sense to realize that it was up to me to fix the situation, regardless of whose fault it was. To recover, I had to reorganize the department, set up new work teams, and begin to meet regularly with the field training staff. By late fall the system was beginning to get back on track, but only through hard work and a painful process of self-discovery. I discovered I was suffering from depression.

For nearly 15 years, I thought I held the upper hand in my battle with Parkinson's disease. My head-on approach had been successful in holding off the worst parts of its physical impact. But I was defenseless against the depression that frequently accompanies PD. Due to my normally aggressive nature, I was always the last person to worry about depression, so I was unable to recognize it when it quietly took over my life. In the past, when other people talked about depression, I had always felt like grabbing them and saying, "Get over it." Now I realize how futile that is when depression has the upper hand.

I had always lived with an upbeat frame of mind. My normal emotional terrain was a high, flat plateau. When the terrain changed and got a little rocky or hilly, I headed for the garage to build something, or went out for a long run. I would run until the endorphins overran my emotions like a dusting of snow, muting the edges of my uneasiness. I'm sometimes amazed at the peaks and valleys of emotion other people, particularly my wife, live with every day. I feel helpless in that terrain. My decision-making has always been ruled by thinking, not feeling. But in 1997, after my successful marathon, I found myself on a very slippery slope. Only now, looking back, can I see how long and steep the decline was. While I was busy fending off the attack on my physical capabilities, Parkinson's silent partner had slipped around back and was taking over the command center. PD, it turns out, is more devious than I suspected.

My problems at work had been developing for three or four years before I was even aware of them. I chose to point the finger at my bosses, or my staff, or at external factors beyond my control, but, since *everything* seemed beyond my control, there were lots of things to blame. My relationship with my assistant manager had deteriorated to the point where we could hardly talk to each other without becoming frustrated and upset. She felt she was working harder and harder, while I was listless, disinterested and going home early. And it wasn't just at work. My confidence had eroded to the point where I began to feel isolated from my family. I didn't believe they cared anymore how I felt or what I thought. I felt uninspired and unsuccessful. Even irrelevant—though that was inevitable, since my children were both teenagers, and therefore programmed by nature to declare me irrelevant. As teenagers, their primary goal in life, of course, was to separate themselves from Edna and me. But since I was already feeling vulnerable, my estrangement from them and from Edna deepened. I felt cut-off and starved for attention. Instead of running toward them, I was running away. It was undoubtedly the dumbest thing I've done as an adult, and it could have cost me everything I cared about in life.

Today I see those feelings of isolation and failure as depression, but at the time I was blind to it. I felt ignored and alone, and so I retreated to the garage where I could actually be alone. I became compulsive about building remote control airplanes. Once built, I would fly them for hours from the hilltops, and crash them repeatedly. Then it was back into the garage to rebuild them, or build something better. Perhaps I felt in control with the airplanes because of their small scale. I was intimidated by larger projects like the back fence that was falling to pieces, or the kitchen I had promised to upgrade. I really wanted to bury myself in a cave, and go into hibernation.

My only safety valve was to throw myself into physical activity, like building airplanes or running the marathon. At least there I had a direct relationship between the energy I put in and the recognition I got back. That made me feel better about myself, but didn't solve my problems at home or at work. And my failure to solve those bigger problems only deepened my depression.

When I began thinking about suicide around October of 1997, I knew I was near the edge. Just driving down the street, I would feel a sudden powerful urge to drift left, into the oncoming lanes of traffic. Standing near the windows of tall buildings, or any high open space, I would suddenly feel an urge to fly. I had experienced that thrill with a hang glider attached to my back, but now I felt an urge to take one long swan dive. Edna and I were in turmoil because of my isolation, and I didn't feel I could talk to her about it. Now I can see I was desperately looking for attention, but unable to ask for it. My behavior was irrational because I wanted to be seen as an honest, hardworking family man, and yet I was dogging it at work, and drawing away from my family, and couldn't see why it was all going so wrong. I hurt my friends at work and my family at home, and they both lost confidence in me.

With Edna's help, I finally admitted I needed professional care, so we went to see a therapist. With both Edna and Dr. Fry helping me, I was able to put a name to the problem: depression. Once I realized what I was dealing with—once I had named it and claimed it for my own—lots of things began to change for the better. I could finally get back to basics.

I started by reassessing my life at work. With my boss's help, I was able to put my management problems in a new context. By admitting that many of the problems at work were the result of my lack of attention, low energy, and falling self-esteem, I was able to stop blaming others for my department's poor performance. It was a classic case of Pogo's [12] important discovery, "We have met the enemy, and he is us!"

Depression made it tough for me to stay on track at work, but my staff rallied around and convinced me that they really did want my leadership. They agreed to help me stay on task, and meet my commitments. My administrative assistant began to keep my daily calendar, and made sure I got to meetings on time. My senior manager offered his continued support for me personally, and for the department. He now understood my Parkinson's symptoms were directly related to my level of stress, and I could not afford to permanently burn myself out in repeated, short-term, all-out efforts. I agreed to tell him when I could no longer handle the stress of managing the department, and he offered to then find or create a position where I could still contribute in my area of expertise.

[12] Walt Kelley's famous cartoon character.

That took a big load off my shoulders, knowing I'd still be able to financially support my family.

Once the problem became clear to them, my children also rallied around, and reassured me that, even though as a parent I could no longer expect to be in control of their lives, they loved me as much as ever. Or as my son put it, "I love you Dad, now may I have the keys to the car?"

This reassurance led to a small breakthrough in my training. All through November, December and January I had been unable to run consistently. I found myself short of breath. I frequently stopped and walked for no apparent reason. Although I knew these problems were caused by depression, I didn't have any defenses for them. I just didn't feel like running. I was still carrying Christmas dinner around my waist in February when I finally reached a turning point. I drove down to Orange County for a half-marathon, thinking I would find the race easily because I ran it the year before. But the start location had been moved several blocks, and by the time I found it, the race had been underway for more than half an hour. I decided just to jog the course, and see if I could find anyone. Under no pressure whatsoever to accomplish anything, I ran without stopping until I caught up to the walkers. I was still comfortable, so I began passing them one-by-one. Eventually, I began catching and passing the slower runners. About mile 7, I caught one of my teammates, and we ran together a little. I ran eight miles without stopping. It was the best run I had had in months. I didn't bother to finish, since I hadn't registered, but I felt good, and I ran relaxed. After that small success, things began to improve.

It was already mid- February when I started training in earnest for the thirteenth L.A. Marathon. During those urgent, intense preparations, I again wrote my thoughts in a journal.

February 17, 1998

Glad the L.A. Marathon is late this year, nearly a month later than the two previous years. We're about six weeks from L.A. XIII, and I've begun the final push. I've been trying to run more consistently, but this shortness of breath continues to be a problem. Still, I have been putting in more miles, with a long run every two weeks or so. Now I need to condense the time frame considerably, because I'm behind schedule.

March 8, 1998

I raised my long run on Saturdays from 10 miles to 12, then 15, 18, and yesterday, with just three weeks left, I ran 19 miles around nine minutes per mile. I'd planned to go for a full three hours, but it just seemed too hard and too hot.

March 15, 1998

I'm collecting money for Students Run L.A.; a charity sponsored by Honda marathon runners. Our goal is to raise enough to buy new running shoes for students in the L.A. City school system who've been training to run the Marathon. Saucony is our partner. They'll contribute high quality running shoes to SRLA for $20 a pair! If we can raise $10,000, Honda's Community Relations department will match it, and with Saucony's help we'll get new running shoes for more than 1000 hard-working kids. But this is about more than running shoes, because during the ten years since SRLA started, nearly 99% of the kids who trained for the marathon have actually gone the full distance. And 95% of those who finished have gone on to finish high school. Compare that to the nearly 40% overall drop-out rate in L.A. city schools! It's incredible to recall myself as a 14-year-old running with Morris and the WARTS, wondering if it would someday be possible for me to run a marathon. I know now the WARTS could have done it, if we had only believed it possible. Through ignorance, we put up so many barriers to our own success. We just didn't believe a 14-year-old had the capacity to run a marathon. In a few days, we'll see more than 1,200 school kids running in the 1998 L.A. Marathon, and most of them will finish. Here's another blinding flash of the obvious: If you believe something is impossible, it is, until somebody else does it.

March 19, 1998

With the race only ten days away, I'm still uncertain. I already said my run last Saturday wasn't quite what I wanted, but forgot to say I worked up a blister on my heel. All my double-layered running socks were dirty, and I just found it too much trouble to do the laundry. I could blame that on my depression, but what difference would it make? The laundry needs doing whether you feel like it or not. Just like the department needs managing whether I feel like it or not. I've still got a lot to learn about dealing with depression.

Training has brought me closer to some of my associates and Running Club teammates. Marathon training treats everyone as equals. Makes no difference whether your job is picking parts in the warehouse or managing a division, you've got to put in the miles to get the result. One of our Club runners, Chieko Allwein, is a 65-year-old who can't weigh more than 85 pounds, and never ran at all until she was in her fifties. Now she's rated at the peak of her age-group. She's probably the Club's best hope of actually winning an age division this year.

March 23, 1998

One week left. The running community is buzzing. My confidence level is up and down. I know this year is different, because in the past I've only been concerned with managing my PD, and this time I have a new adversary. I'm sure my stubborn efforts to stay fit have helped maintain my physical ability, but I don't know how much the depression will affect me. Of one thing I'm certain: I would take the same approach next time if I had the chance to do it again. Of course, I can't go back, and live life differently to compare the outcomes. We only get one chance. Let's try to get it right the first time. So what have I concluded? That strength and fitness can overcome many complications in life. It benefits everyone, even the healthy.

March 24, 1998

Nothing ever goes quite the way you hoped, does it? I did everything I could to be healthy and ready for the marathon, and now, with less than a week to go, I'm down with an earache. I went out on my final long practice run yesterday, but it was a struggle. I ran about ten miles up Turnbull Canyon and back, but the ear infection left me feeling weak. I keep telling myself: "No one ever said this was supposed to be easy. It's just another obstacle to overcome. I've done the miles, my mental state is improved, I know what I've done before, and I have help from my running partners. Why should I let an earache get in the way?"

March 25, 1998

I'm on my way to Chicago for a training conference, and I know I'm putting next Sunday's performance in jeopardy. I seldom sleep well or eat properly on business trips, so I'm not making it easy on myself. But at least the doctor treated the ear infection, and insisted I'd be fully recovered before the race.

March 30, 1998

The day after…I'm tired, stiff and sore, but about as happy as anyone has a right to be. I finished my third L.A. Marathon, not as fast as I'd hoped, but fast enough to feel like I gave it my best. The weather cooperated with a spectacularly clear Los Angeles morning. The day started out cool, not raining and windy like the day before. The event organizers got almost everything they asked for, except a really fast time. They wanted to upgrade L.A.'s image by increasing the prize and appearance money for the elite men and women in the quest for a fast winning time, but the course is just too hard. The winner's time of 2:11 will not look like much to the international press, but those of us who ran it know how tough this course is.

Our club had some great achievements, including quite a few personal bests. Michael finished 100th overall. His wife, Alicia, ran a personal record of 3 hours, 56 minutes, and *her first time under 4 hours in several tries. And Chieko won for women over 65 with an incredible 4:08! Overall, Honda finished first in the corporate competition, beating Boeing for the first time. The four-hour group fell apart early because we started much too far back in the huge mass of runners and walkers. After the gun, it took nearly ten minutes to get to the starting line, and by then the group had split up. There were just too many bodies to get by as a group. I was slower than I expected, but I'm happy to have finished, after a bad start.*

When Edna and I were packing for the hotel the night before the race, my brother called to wish me luck. I was reaching for my runner's number bib and the special electronic chip—worn on one shoe to capture start and finish times— when I picked up the phone, so in my mind I'd already put both things in the bag. At the hotel the next morning, I got up, got dressed, and reached into my bag for the number bib, but it wasn't there. Yet I was certain I'd brought it, and then I remembered the phone call. I thought, "Jim, you always were a problem for me!" I wasn't being fair, of course. He'd called to give his love and support, not to create a diversion. Called Sarah at 7 am and asked her to bring me the number bib and chip. She made it in time, and found me at the underground trolley station. I owe her a big "thanks" for the effort. Made it to the starting grid with the rest of our group, but my early morning stress took me out of my game plan—the anxiety made it tough to get my medications balanced.

I struggled through the early miles, couldn't find a groove. Tom stayed with me to help, but it just wasn't in the cards for the day. The temperature went from hot in the sun to freezing in the shade; it was easy to get chilled in the shady parts of the course. The day began to drag when I realized I wasn't going to be even close to my target time, but I never lost sight of finishing. We were a couple miles past mid-point before I could convince Tom I wouldn't be dropping out, and it was okay for him to go at his own pace. Apparently he'd promised himself not to abandon me. Took some time, but he finally ran on to join the others.

Could I have forgotten how long a marathon really is? Running miles 17 through 23 reminded me! And I realized that running with the 4 and ½-hour group is different from running with the 4 hour group. You have to run to get under four hours, but at 4 and ½ you're surrounded by the walking wounded. I saw several examples of what I'd feared as a child, when I thought of the marathon as a survival test. All around me, runners could only walk, or trot at best. Most had started out well, but had now "hit the wall." Many were limping badly due to blisters or cramps, while others were just lying alongside the road. A few were getting medical help. Everywhere I looked, I saw faces distorted with pain. Thankfully, the crowds were tremendously encouraging, and each runner who recovered enough to get going again was met with a huge ovation. In mile 23 I caught up with another of our Honda team runners; I could see he was suffering badly from cramps in his calves. For once, I was able to forget about my own time; I stayed with him, and concentrated on his making it to the finish. I understood then that my wife is right when she says, "Nothing happens totally by chance." Maybe it was just my turn to give some help, instead of always receiving it. I know I gave the race an honest effort, and we both finished with our heads held high.

As we neared the bottom of the last downhill on Wilshire Boulevard before the turn to the finish, I heard Edna, David, and Sarah shouting encouragement. Sarah got so enthusiastic she broke through the restraints, and ran out in the street to cheer me on. David and Edna followed. I was so happy to have them there. They'd been waiting more than two hours, cheering for all my teammates. There was an incredible sense of joy and accomplishment as I crossed the finish line. Los Angeles was sharp-edged and sparkling from yesterday's rain, the sky was bright blue, and the breeze was cool and fresh. That's probably as close to heaven as you can get while still on earth. "Just another perfect day," as Randy Newman sings in his anthem to L.A.

It was a great event for the company, and for the Running Club. After the race, Honda provided a hospitality suite with sandwiches, cookies, and ice cream sundaes. As each new finisher came in, they were greeted with a big round of applause from their peers, and handed a large, fresh and fluffy towel to collapse on. I was extremely proud of all the runners and walkers who finished, and proud of my family just for being part of the event. I rediscovered that nothing is more important than family. The boundary between who is and is not "family" may be a little vague, but right now it stretches way out into the community.

Chapter 12
Getting Connected

I did finally connect with the community of support groups for people with Parkinson's. My running brought me to the attention of support group leaders, and gave me a message to share with others in my situation. I began to feel connected to the Parkinson's community as a whole, but I seldom connected with the individuals in it because they were all so much older, and with more advanced symptoms. Then I found a "Young Onset" support group in the Beverly Hills area, and realized there were now a lot of people with PD who were younger than I was! They were active, had careers and young children and aging parents to worry about. I began thinking I could be too old for this group. In fact, I'd been living with the disease for so long I was too old to be called a "young onsetter." Edna and I had already worked our way through many of their concerns, but that gave us something to share with them.

At one Young Onset group meeting, Edna and I heard about the Parkinson's Action Network. We discovered that PAN was taking an active role in trying to shape a national policy toward Parkinson's. The leader of PAN was Joan Samuelson, a young California attorney with PD, and a dynamic voice on Capitol Hill, a constant force behind legislative action, and a compelling face in front of congress. PAN put together conferences in Washington, D.C. to teach PD patients to advocate for themselves, so they could get their faces and stories into the heads of their elected representatives. PAN invited scientists and patient advocates to work together to shape the thinking in Congress. Representative Morris Udall had died from Parkinson's, and Samuelson found support in congress from his friends. She worked diligently on the Udall Bill which earmarked money within the budget of the National Institutes of Health (NIH) for studying Parkinson's disease, and authorized the creation of Udall Centers around the country for research and patient support services. PAN, with Joan Samuelson at the helm, got the Udall Bill passed in 1997.

Then in 1998, Michael J. Fox announced he had Parkinson's disease, and suddenly it was okay to talk about having it, not just with fellow sufferers and doctors and support groups, but with society at large. Michael Fox decided to leave his successful TV show *Spin City* to become a Parkinson's disease advocate. He formed the Michael J. Fox Foundation, and merged it with The Parkinson's Action Network. Edna and I went to our first PAN conference in 2000, where Michael J. Fox overwhelmed attendees with his presence. Joan Samuelson and PAN were suddenly submerged in the wake of his celebrity status. Edna and I were caught up in the action, standing in the banquet hall after dinner while Michael circled the entire ballroom, shaking hands with everyone in the room, listening to their stories, sharing their fears, smiling at their successes. We had come to Washington to learn how to be advocates for Parkinson's disease research, and left with the impression that with Fox's help, there was nothing to stop us from finding its cause and a cure. Dr. Fishbach, head of the NIH, had announced to the world that with proper funding, scientists could have a cure for Parkinson's in five to ten years. Congress asked the NIH to make plans for developing a cure. The NIH then responded, saying they would need a doubled budget for the next 5 years, and funding of $15 billion dedicated to research on Parkinson's. With that support they would also be contributing to the search for cures of other degenerative neurological diseases such as Alzheimer's and ALS.

Edna and I returned from the PAN conference convinced we should do more than just take care of our family. We felt a kinship with others in the Parkinson's community that drove us to get involved, to speak out, and to help those who were suffering more than we were. We moved our target from community support to advocacy.

My first 12 years with Parkinson's were spent just dealing with personal issues—learning to live with PD, and adapting to the ways it reduced my capabilities. That was phase one. Then I discovered my family was also living with the disease, and adjusting to my adaptations. This second phase moved me from my personal concerns to family concerns, from isolation to sharing. Then, running marathons moved me into a third phase of understanding: Parkinson's is a community disease. Its effects extend beyond the individual sufferer and his family to all of society. After writing the article on running the marathon for the National Parkinson Foundation newsletter, I found opportunities to participate in fund-raising events and support groups. Working with Kim Seidman of the National Parkinson Foundation, I helped organize a 5K run for PD, and spoke to other PD patients at several support-group meetings. I had moved from isolation to sharing, and from sharing to support. Now, after the PAN conference, I moved from support to action. I wanted to be an advocate.

Thanks to the Internet, I found I could stay connected to the community. In late 1998, I began lurking on the PD patient's Open Forum hosted by the National Parkinson Foundation. At first I sat on the sidelines, content to read the dialog. I watched as newly diagnosed patients wrote to the forum, full of fear and misunderstanding, and often anger and denial. And then a chorus of experienced voices answered, full of care, wisdom, and understanding to educate the ignorant and reassure the fearful.

The NPF forum has three other "channels" that offer: 1) a meeting place for caregivers, 2) advice from a Movement Disorder Specialist, Dr. Abe Lieberman, on "Ask the Doctor," and 3) advice from a dietician, Kathrynne Holden, on "Ask the Dietician." Although they don't participate directly in the patient forum, both Dr. Leiberman and Ms. Holden are referred to and quoted frequently by members of the patient forum. They are very important resources, and far more than competent; they are really on top of what's happening right now and diligent in answering tough questions.

The NPF Open Forum is a wonderful resource that helps many new patients and caregivers find answers to their toughest questions, and comfort for their deepest fears. Each of these voices has helped many newly diagnosed PWPs and their families, and also each other, since they routinely come back to the forum for help with their own issues. Discussion threads repeat occasionally, but always with some variation. And the archive of discussion threads lets newcomers research past discussions without intruding on current dialog. Some threads discuss the social and political issues affecting the Parkinson's community. Religion and politics cannot, and probably should not, be avoided because Parkinson's is a community disease, and the community must be free to talk about everything that affects living with PD, including philosophical, ethical, religious and political beliefs.

Occasionally, someone will take exception to a comment on the forum, sometimes due to a misunderstanding, but most often because the comment involved a political statement or a religious belief. We're living in a complex world, coping with a complex disease, and ethics, religion, and politics affect how this disease is understood and treated.

As the presidential campaign got underway in 2004, there was a dispute that nearly silenced the forum for a while; it started out with a joke. It was a political joke that mocked liberal democrats and brought out the worst on both sides of the discussion. I'm afraid it was an accurate reflection of the deepening division between conservatives and liberals within our society. After the initial joke, there were several responses that took the name-calling and branding to ever lower levels until several members of the forum threatened to quit forever. Many called out for a return to Parkinson's subjects only, and to stay away from all non-related subjects. Distracted by the disputes, we really did lose our way on the forum for a short time, but finally we were able to recover our momentum and direction. There are many intelligent and strong-minded people among the Parkinson's community who value this forum and won't let it die.

There are also many caring and forgiving souls in the group who support everyone's right to express themselves, and are willing to discuss any issue, regardless of political or religious content, that may affect our community.

Fortunately, the NPF Open Forum survived the election and is currently healthy and available to anyone who has an interest or need to learn more about Parkinson's disease. We frequently find students dropping in to learn about the disease for class assignments, and they find a knowledgeable and articulate assortment of patients, with experience ranging from just a few months to many years, that are willing to share their feelings as well as their knowledge.

Although the patient forum has many individual voices, I must name a few because of unique differences in their character. I've used their Internet names - not to protect their personal identities – but simply because in many cases that's all I know. They may seem faceless because the Internet is still a print medium for the most part, but these are real people who've lived with Parkinson's for many years, and have learned to cope with its challenges: Chaplain Brian, Nancy the Wise, Jim (AKA Silverfoxx), ADANCR, Maronij, Tenacity Wins, Tondeleyo, Kalalau4, PetewithPD (now known as PetehealedofPD), JoJoBean, Marie, Aunti Ji, and SusieCoQ10.

You can count on these voices when you need information or advice. Chaplain Brian is kind and caring, a thoughtful man who never asserts his own views over anyone else's, yet is willing to question and probe deeply into many subject areas. Nancy the Wise is always writing tragic-comic stories about how Parkinson's turns ordinary events into extraordinary humor. Jim (AKA Silverfoxx) is a true survivor, always challenging the skeptics, who's given us a great account of his DBS surgery. Tondeleyo is strong and usually upbeat, and Tenacity Wins has survived the wildest roller coaster ride I ever heard of, yet still finds time to help others understand the technology associated with PD. Kalalau4 is our poet-in-residence, although he must occasionally share that title with Chaplain Brian, JoJoBean, and Aunti Ji. An amazing amount of poetry appears on this forum. JoJo is our lead comic and just a rhyming fool. She can turn anything into a source of amusement through her earthy approach to language. Aunti Ji, who earned her nickname in India where she lived for several years as a missionary, brings her caring spirit and soothing voice to some of our more heated discussions. But among all these voices, the one *everyone* listens to and trusts is "Maronij." Her real name is Joan, but she acquired the nickname "Maronij" from a rhyming pop song when her sister called her "Boney Maroni Joanie" which was then shortened to "Maronij". The nickname stuck, and eventually became her Internet name. I thought at first it sounded exotic, probably East Indian, and pictured a dark, sharp-eyed, sooth-saying goddess with multiple arms. We've never met so I can't verify that image, but it stays with me because Maronij certainly has a sharp eye for the truth, a willingness to speak her mind, and her hands are busy stirring many different pots. She's a voracious reader of the medical literature on Parkinson's, and has a way of translating her knowledge and personal experience into practical advice. To me she represents the "earth mother" of the Parkinson's patient community. She pays attention to her disease, understands her own experience, and shares her ideas and advice without being bossy.

Finally, I must say that occasionally we lose an important voice on the forum, and we certainly did so in the fall of 2004: Joan Hartman passed away. When I first began paying attention to the forum, hers was one of the voices I paid most attention to because she was open, warm and knowledgeable. Gradually her posts on the forum diminished until we heard from her only occasionally. And now we will hear from her no more. Her passing brought home to me how very strange and special internet relationships can be. Prior to the internet, I would not have imagined the kind of relationship I now share with so many people I've never even seen. The internet removes barriers and allows us to share ideas quickly at a very personal level; it's an opportunity to really get inside people's heads and understand their hearts – with no limits in time or space. The channel is open 24/7, anywhere in the world.

A few months after joining the forum, I suggested we try turning our "Parkie Dialogs" into a book. The forum members responded enthusiastically, but I ended up working on *this* book instead! For two reasons, first, I couldn't nail down the subject matter of the forum because it was constantly evolving and reshaping itself, as I expect it will do until the day we are all free of this disease. Second, I found a great book that described a lot of the forum's concerns, and included issues and examples from another Parkinson's forum, called the Parkinson's Information Exchange Network (PIEN). That book is <u>When Parkinson's Strikes Early</u>, by Barbara Blake-Krebs and Linda Herman.[13] This book is a great resource for people with Parkinson's as well as for caregivers and family. But it can't take the place of daily contact with other forum members, and the opportunity to give—and sometimes get—help.

One subject area that the forum has avoided to some degree is the current debate on embryonic stem cells. But it's an important discussion, and one that may have a huge impact on the future treatment of Parkinson's and other neurodegenerative diseases, including Amyotrophic Lateral Sclerosis (ALS, also know as Lou Gehrig's disease), and Huntington's disease. Together with gene therapy, stem cells may be the pathway to curing some of mankind's oldest and most devastating chronic diseases.

Gene replacement therapy is the focus of research on diseases caused by genetic defects. According to the Dana Alliance for Brain Initiatives, "Gene therapy, in which the brain's own systems for cell growth are harnessed to combat brain illnesses, is a promising area of brain research. The idea is to introduce into people, genes that can compensate for functions lost through disease or injury."[14] But doctors and scientists have reached no conclusion regarding what percentage of Parkinson's stems from genetic predisposition and what percentage from environmental factors. There do appear to be a few large cohorts of Parkinson's sufferers within specific families,

---

[13] Blake-Krebs, Barbara, and Herman, Linda, When Parkinson's Strikes Early: Voices, Choices, Resources and Treatment, Hunter House Publishers, Alameda, California, 2001.

[14] "Staying Sharp: current advances in brain research: Chronic Health Issues", AARP Foundation and the Dana Alliance for Brain Initiatives, NY, NY, 2004.

but there are some differences between the symptoms these people express and those of the typical idiopathic Parkinson's.

In 2002, I submitted a sample of my DNA to a long-term study of Parkinson's patients conducted by the National Institutes of Health in an attempt to identify any genetic markers for PD, but I have not been informed as to the results of that study. I hope that I will someday, because I would like to let my children know if they are the carriers of such a marker, and both David and Sarah have told me they would prefer to know if they bear a damaged or faulty gene likely to cause Parkinson's. A genetic component of Parkinson's has not been ruled out, and study of several genes that are associated with Parkinson's, such as Parkin and Alpha-synuclein will continue.

Most Parkinson's researchers believe a combination of genetic factors and environmental toxins is the most likely cause of the disease. Consequently, they are focused on both gene therapy—because it can provide new directions to correct defective processes, and on stem cells—because of their potential to become other types of cells, and then replace damaged cells of a specific type anywhere in the body. Stem cells are those non-differentiated cells in the earliest stages of an embryo that later become specific cell types to form muscles, nerves, bones, blood and the organs of the body. It turns out that there are also adult stem cells, found in blood from the umbilical cord and placenta, in bone marrow, muscle, fat, the brain, and many other parts of the body. Although initially they were not believed to be as flexible as the embryonic stem cells (ESC), adult stem cells (ASC) have been an important subject of study for potential treatments and cures, and have already demonstrated some success. As I write this, an on-going concern over the use of embryonic stem cells has turned these two stem cell types into competitors, and their supporters and even researchers into opposing factions. Scientific study is continuing on both types, but efforts are underway to limit study on embryonic cells to existing stem cell lines (current policy of the Bush administration) and/or frozen embryos due to be discarded, so it's important to understand how embryonic and adult cells differ, and how scientists acquire them.

As an embryo grows, its stem cells continue replicating for about fourteen days before they begin to form specific organs or cell types. At present, scientists are unable to remove the stem cells from the embryo without destroying it. Currently, embryonic stem cells are harvested primarily from embryos left over from in-vitro fertilization (IVF). In the future they may come from therapeutic cloning, also known as somatic cell nuclear transfer (SCNT), a process used by South Korean researchers in early 2004 to produce the first cloned human embryos. IVF is used in fertility clinics for people who want to have children but are not able to naturally. The IVF process creates embryos by mixing a woman's eggs with a man's sperm in a lab dish. One (or more) of the resulting embryos is then implanted in the mother's womb. Any embryos left over are frozen for possible future use. There are fertility clinics throughout the U.S., and each of them may have several thousand frozen embryos waiting to be implanted or eventually discarded. According to Steve Meyer of the Stem Cell Action Network (SCAN) there may be as many as 400,000 frozen embryos presently stored in clinics across the country. How long these embryos can remain viable while frozen is not presently known.

Cloning/SCNT can be either "reproductive"—making a "genetic copy" of someone, which many countries have banned, or "therapeutic"—creating an embryo so its stem cells can be harvested and used for therapeutic purposes, including research into cures for disease. For cloning/SCNT, the nucleus is removed from an egg and replaced with the nucleus of a donor cell with its complete set of 46 chromosomes, and then a mild electrical shock is applied to the egg to stimulate cell division. The resulting embryo grows in the same way as an embryo resulting from a normally fertilized egg. This is the process that produced the sheep Dolly, the first successfully cloned mammal. What would a fully developed human clone be like? We don't know—a cloned human embryo has never been successfully implanted, brought to term, and born. The purpose of therapeutic cloning/SCNT, however, is not to produce a human clone, but to produce stem cells that genetically match the cells of someone with chronic disease or injury so the stem cells can replace any damaged cells without risk of rejection. Although some people are fearful that this SCNT technology could be misused to create masses of mutant humanoids, or replicate replacement bodies of some powerful political figure, the notion of the mad scientist trying to control the world is as out of date as the pulp fiction that created the image. Stem cell research is being placed under public oversight and scientific controls, such as California's Institute for Regenerative Medicine (the outcome of Prop 71) and the National Institutes of Health (NIH) so it will be monitored to ensure ethical applications of the resulting technology.

Adult stem cells are found in many organs of our bodies and may be isolated and harvested without destroying the organ or tissue. They have many of the capabilities of embryonic stem cells, but their own programming limits them to becoming only certain cell types in the body. Researchers have, however, also treated or manipulated them to become cells other than the type they might normally replenish. Although adult stem cells are being used in experimental treatments for diseases, the mechanism behind their regenerative effect is still not clear, but it seems to occur in at least three different ways: 1) "interconversion" between different tissue types, known as transdifferentiation, or 2) fusion of the adult stem cells with the host tissue, taking on that tissue's characteristics, or 3) not contributing directly to tissue regeneration, but instead stimulating the targeted tissues to begin their own repair. Whatever the regenerative mechanism is, treatment with adult stem cells is similar to a bone marrow transplant. Adult stem cells of the type related to the damaged tissue are harvested from the patient. In the lab, once the stem cells grow and differentiate, they are sorted and cells that match the damaged cells are then transplanted back into the patient where they integrate into the target tissue, and begin functioning normally. A recent experimental treatment for Parkinson's disease used this technique on one patient.[15]

Those who favor research on adult stem cells point to their current use in promising experimental treatments for more than 50 diseases,

---

[15] Information on Dr. Levesque's treatment can be found at: http://commerce.senate.gov/hearings/witnesslist.cfm?id=1268.

as well as the discovery of more types of adult stem cells than were previously thought to exist, and the ability of adult stem cells to become other types of cells, something scientists once thought only embryonic stem cells could do. Many in this group also support adult stem cell research because it avoids the ethical and religious issues raised by using embryonic stem cells—no embryo needs to be created and destroyed, and no eggs need to be taken from women donors.

Those who favor research on embryonic stem cells point to the fact that as an embryo develops, its stem cells become all the other types of cells in the body. So, if scientists can find out what controls that process of cell differentiation, they may be able to trigger stem cells to become a specific type of body cell, and use them to replace any cells in the body that have been damaged by disease or injury. They may also be able to regenerate entire organs, possibly in response to instructions from reprogrammed or reactivated genes. Simply implanting undifferentiated embryonic stem cells in damaged tissue has proved unreliable, and sometimes produces tumors. It is obviously premature to attempt such strategies without understanding the control mechanisms that govern cell, tissue, and organ development.

Since the embryo is destroyed in the current process of harvesting its stem cells, ESC research is at odds with a variety of people and religious groups that essentially believe every embryo, no matter how it was conceived, is not only a unique human being from the moment of conception, but also a spiritual being created by God, in his image. Although scientists, theologians and laity may disagree about whether God exists or men have souls, that's not the real heart of the stem cell discussion. This is not a contest between religion and science. Religion is a matter of transcendent belief, apart from the material world, and won't be "proved" or "disproved" by scientific study. I think it is pointless to set science and religion as antagonists in this discussion, because I believe both science and religion are essential to humanity. In my frame of reference, science is the tool we use to understand God's creation. Scientists agree that the embryos used to obtain embryonic stem cells, if implanted in a woman's uterus, could grow into a human being, but many scientists and ethicists agree that the embryo (or blastocyst as it is called in the first fourteen days of undifferentiated activity) does not require protection in the earliest stage of its development because it's not yet fully human. I'm comfortable with this understanding, and therefore support embryonic, as well as adult stem cell research. And I'm confident in the scientific rigor and ethics being applied to the study of both embryonic and adult stem cells.

For those who believe every embryo, regardless of how it is conceived, is fully human this course of action will remain an ethical problem. Indeed, some scientists and doctors who study and treat human reproductive problems have deep concerns about the in-vitro fertilization process used by fertility clinics. Doctors in the clinics normally collect and fertilize several eggs from each patient, but only implant one or two at a time. The rest are kept frozen in case they may be needed later. This process routinely produces several hundred or even thousands of frozen fertilized eggs in each clinic. Most scientists interested in researching embryonic stem cells believe these embryos, which will otherwise be kept frozen or discarded, eventually could provide any additional stem cell lines needed for basic research.

One idea that may resolve these concerns is a proposal to disable one or more genes in the nucleus of the donor cell before inserting it in the egg. Then when the electrical current is applied, the egg cell would begin dividing, form the stem cells, and then stop dividing because of the "gap" in its genetic instructions. The individual stem cells could then be harvested and cultured from a non-viable embryo This, of course, raises another question: How is disabling a gene in the body cell nucleus, in effect "pre-programming" the resulting embryo to self-destruct, different from destroying a viable embryo by harvesting its stem cells? For those who believe the embryo is fully human from the moment of conception, the essential question seems to be: Can embryonic stem cells be created without creating or destroying an embryo?

Views on stem cell research are diverse enough to divide politicians, even within the same party: Republican Senator Orin

Hatch of Utah, for example, is pro-life, an elder in the Mormon Church, and has written about his acceptance of the need to study embryonic stem cells in his book, Square Peg: Confessions of a Citizen Senator. Senator Hatch spent several months agonizing over the subject and concluded that "If successful, stem cell research could liberate not only the sick but their families as well."[16] Furthermore, he concluded that "Having the research financed by government will help ensure that appropriate limits are (maintained.)"[17] After studying the issue in depth, he reached the conclusion that research into embryonic stem cells should continue, with government support, using IVF embryos that would otherwise be discarded.

U.S. Senate Majority Leader Bill Frist of Tennessee, who is pro-life, a Presbyterian, and the only physician in the Senate, agrees with Senator Hatch on providing funding for ESC research on leftover IVF embryos. But Frist would ban the creation of embryos solely for research, and continue the ban on funding for deriving stem cells from embryos, but increase funding for research on ASCs.

U.S. Senator Sam Brownback of Kansas who is pro-life, a Roman Catholic and former attorney, and chairs the Commerce Subcommittee on Science, Technology, and Space believes the use of cloning/SCNT in research should be banned, and ASC research, because of its promising results, should be funded much more heavily. He has also proposed legislation to criminalize the use of cloning/ SCNT in any research that involves or affects interstate commerce, or the importation of an embryo. Individual states, however, could still allow or prohibit cloning/SCNT within their borders. The proposed Act (S-245 or H.R. 2505) does not restrict using SCNT or other cloning techniques to produce molecules, DNA, cells or tissue (except for human embryos), organs, plants, or animals (except for humans).

This debate will continue, in Congress and across the country . . . as it should. Basic science and research is not focused on producing salable products and is therefore normally funded through NIH's

---

[16] Hatch, Orrin G., Square Peg: Confessions of a Citizen Senator, Basic Books, NY, NY, 2002, page 247.

[17] Hatch, Orrin G., op cit, page 246.

allocation of public funds. Therefore, it is important that everyone from politicians, researchers, and investors to doctors, patients, and taxpayers clearly understand the issues involved.

Embryonic stem cell research will likely be centered in California where voters have approved Proposition 71, a three billion dollar bond issue to support both ESC and ASC research. Because of the passage of Prop 71, several other states including New Jersey, Illinois and Wisconsin have also established or are considering their own stem cell institutes. California's new Institute for Regenerative Medicine assures funding for both types of stem cells, so the differences between them may become less important than how much money will be allocated for research on which diseases. We know there are significant challenges to the successful management of this bond issue, but we in the Parkinson's community have backed Joan Samuelson, President of PAN, to become a member of the Independent Citizen's Oversight Committee (ICOC), because she not only knows our needs as a patient community, and knows the political landscape on which decisions will be made, but she is also ethical and caring and, above all, wants to do the "right thing" for the future of mankind. Fortunately, our recommendations were heard, and she was appointed to the ICOC at its formation.

Chapter 13

The Formation of Team Parkinson

In March 1999, Mary Yost was among more than a million spectators lining the streets of L.A. for the marathon. She was standing on Sunset Boulevard near the 22-mile mark of the race with several colleagues from her job at UCLA to cheer on a friend, Annie Love. Annie had been talking about running the marathon for several months, and had piqued Mary's interest in it. Mary was also there to cheer for her nephew, Thomas Provost, who was running his second marathon. It was almost noon and the racers had been streaming by her for at least 2 hours already, and, although she wasn't looking for me, she saw me approaching, and shouted my name. I was so surprised; I stopped, looked around, and saw Mary, whom I recognized from a Parkinson's advocacy conference a few months earlier. She looked small behind her large round glasses, and slightly stooped from her ten years of living with Parkinson's. Since I was running my fourth L.A. Marathon, and was no longer concerned with finish times or placings, I ran over and gave her a big sweaty hug and a little kiss on the cheek! I think she understood how much the race meant to me. She seemed proud of me, but I was proud of her too, because I knew how hard it was for her just to be there, standing in one spot for so long. When you've got PD, standing still can be more difficult than running because it consumes more dopamine. It's actually much easier to keep moving. I thanked Mary for being there, and then ran on to the finish.

Mary was inspired and energized by the marathon. She was surprised to see such huge groups of children as well as a group of 80 year-olds going by. A young woman ran by on an artificial leg, followed a few minutes later by a man on crutches, with a roller skate on his single leg. She was utterly amazed, and said to her friends, "Until you actually come out and watch a marathon, you have no idea such a wide variety of people actually do it." Standing by the curb, Mary recalled that a few years earlier Kim Seidman had mentioned some guy with Parkinson's who ran marathons, but she couldn't believe it. Now, after a sweaty hug and a kiss on the cheek, she thought, "Why can't I do that? All it takes is putting one foot in front of the other." She had made her decision.

Mary committed herself to walking the next L.A. Marathon. Her nephew Tom agreed to help her, and they both signed up to train with the L.A. Roadrunners. Next, she began to think of all the ways she might assist the Parkinson's community through her commitment to the marathon. She was an active leader in the L.A. Metro Young Onset Parkinson's group, and had worked in Washington, D.C. on getting the Udall Bill passed, so she was no stranger to taking direct action. In June 1999, she wrote an email to the L.A. Marathon asking if the Young Parkinson's group could be added to the list of charities they sponsor, but got no response. Then in October she got a call from the marathon's charity coordinator. "We've got a couple of openings," she said, "and you're under consideration to become one of our Official Charities. We'll need your proposal in 3 to 4 days."

The Young-Onset Parkinson's group was then struggling with internal challenges. Mary was still working full-time in the Physics department at UCLA, and also training for the marathon, so she called the local coordinators of the National Parkinson's Foundation and the American Parkinson Disease Association for help. Neither office could take on the project. She then called Carol Walton, her mentor when she'd worked on the Udall Bill. Mary liked Carol because of her persistence, patience, energy, and hard work. Carol had recently been hired as Executive Director of The Parkinson

Alliance, headquartered in Princeton, New Jersey, and was in the process of moving there from California. She offered to support the idea, and suggested Mary talk to Ken Aidekman, a Parkinson's advocate, and co-founder of the Parkinson's Unity Walk in New York City. Mary liked the idea of linking the New York City Unity Walk to Team Parkinson in L.A. so she called Ken and asked, "What if we were to grab that last slot? What could we do as an official charity of the marathon?" Ken was skeptical at first, but agreed to review her proposal.

Mary had to give the Marathon committee an answer in a couple of days, so she pulled an all-nighter, threw the proposal together, and sent it overnight to Ken and his Unity Walk co-founder, Margot Zobel. Ken and Margot made some revisions to the proposal, and sent it back to Mary the same day. Mary agreed to the changes, and delivered the proposal to the Marathon office on her lunch break, just in time. The proposal read in part:

> ...*The spirit of our group matches exactly the spirit of your race, which succeeds so well in promoting unity in the world's most diverse city. One goal drives us forward: Cure Parkinson's disease. We are committed to raising money for research to achieve our goal...Our annual event in New York City's Central Park has given us the experience needed to expand our horizons. The L.A. Marathon would be the ideal opportunity.*

A week later the proposal was accepted, and Team Parkinson became a partner of the Unity Walk, with The Parkinson Alliance providing administrative support, as well as tax exempt charity status under paragraph 501(c)(3) of the Internal Revenue Code.

In December of 1999, Mary hosted a meeting at her house to set up the project and divide up the work. Edna and I were eager to help, but didn't know most of the other players. I knew Kim Seidman, of course, because we'd planned a 5k run in Griffith Park, and I recognized Susan Kline and Rod Preston because I'd met them at a Young-Onset Parkinson's group. Newcomers included:

Mignone Trenary from the Orange County Chapter of the National Parkinson's Foundation, Ken Aidekman who was there from New York representing the Unity Walk, and Carol Walton who was there just days after moving from California to New Jersey to take up her new job with The Parkinson Alliance.

Edna and I listened patiently through most of the meeting, although I found it difficult to keep quiet. As far as I knew, we were the only ones in the room who were familiar with the marathon. And no one else in the room had actually run one. Then the Quality of Life Expo came up for discussion. After three years of attending the Expo, we knew it was an important part of the marathon experience in L.A. Still, it caught me by surprise when Edna spontaneously volunteered to pay the $500 it cost to get a booth! She wanted to honor her mother who had recently passed away. I was proud of her for that, not only because it meant she really understood how the marathon worked, but also because of her generosity.

A ton of work had to be done to get Team Parkinson running in just three months. Most of the organizing work fell to Mignone Trenary in California and Margot Zobel in New York. Without their dedication and zeal, I doubt we would have been there on race day. Although Mary Yost focused much of her energy on preparing to run in the marathon, she was always looking for opportunities to share the idea of Team Parkinson. Mary trained with the L.A. Roadrunners, so she invited me to run with them one Saturday morning, and Coach Connally gave me a few minutes to pitch Team Parkinson to their huge training group. We didn't recruit many team members that morning, but at least we got our name out there, and handed out a few brochures. I got a kick out of the looks on some faces when I told them I'd had PD for 20 years, and was going to run my fourth marathon!

In spite of impossible timelines and clueless committee members like me, Team Parkinson was there on March 4, 2000 for the Acura Bike Tour, the L.A. Marathon, and the 5K walk. Most of the credit goes to Margot, Mignone and her partner Tom Brown, as well as Mary and my wife Edna. Many others contributed time and effort to the fundraising, particularly Kathleen Cooper-Burton. I didn't know it at the time, but Kathleen had been a big fundraiser for PD in the 1980s and 1990s, and we were fortunate to have her as part of Team Parkinson. But the core group of Mignone, Tom, Margo and Mary had prepared the brochure, banners, posters and signs, and Linda Squires-O'Connor enlisted the volunteers for the Expo. Turning the L.A. Marathon into a charity fundraiser takes a lot of people. Edna and I worked at the Expo preparing for race-day activities; Edna also worked with Sheralyn Richardson of the National Parkinson's Foundation to set up the Team Parkinson cheering station.

On race day, I knew at least three people with Parkinson's would be in the Acura Bike Tour riding for Team Parkinson: Tom Brown, Ted Bean and Jim Wetherell, whose motto is "I never give up!" Ken Aidekman would join them on a bike he borrowed from me. I got a little nervous when I noticed the bike didn't fit him very well; it's almost too big for me, and he's a couple of inches shorter than I am. I was also concerned that he was riding without proper shoes, and I didn't have time to get the snap-in pedals off. If his foot slipped off the pedal, his crotch could hit the crossbar. Ouch! I didn't know if he'd already had kids, but I didn't want to be responsible if later he found he couldn't! I knew only that his father had died with Parkinson's, and that Ken was somehow connected to a foundation that financially supported the Parkinson's Action Network. I was surprised such an important guy would willingly ride on an oversized, borrowed bike without the proper shoes. Since I've gotten to know Ken better over the years, I've come to expect surprises.

Two of us with PD officially entered the Marathon that day, along with several healthy team members running for family members and friends. In total, about 25 runners and walkers ran the marathon for Team Parkinson that first year. The 5k walk was also loaded with joggers and walkers from Team Parkinson, including Margot Zobel who also has PD, and is co-founder with Ken Aidekman of the Unity Walk in New York. By the weekend of its first marathon, Team Parkinson had grown to nearly 80 members.

Being at The Quality of Life Expo brought us face-to-face with the marathon audience, and we enlisted nearly 20 new runners for Team Parkinson. Without the booth, they would never have heard about us. And we got a little public relations help when Tim McClune interviewed me during the race. Tim is a light-hearted newsman who runs the marathon with a microphone in hand and a motorcycle-based TV crew at his heels, interviewing runners throughout the race. He's genuinely funny, sometimes poking fun at the people he interviews, but he did our interview with a great deal of grace, and kept it focused on the issues of running with PD. The interview aired about two-thirds through the day's broadcast, even though we'd taped it at the first mile. The early taping was nice for two reasons: because I was fresh and looked good—when the tape was shown three hours later in the broadcast, people were amazed at how strongly I was running! And because it was just starting to rain—once it got started, I thought it would never stop.

L.A. Marathon XV was run in one of the worst downpours ever to hit Los Angeles. Several inches of rain fell throughout the day, and it was windy and cold (by Southern California standards). Actually it wasn't all that bad for a marathon runner (no worries about overheating or dehydration), if you didn't mind the ankle-deep water, but it was terrible for spectators. Several times, deep water forced our Team Parkinson Cheering Station to abandon their post at Mile 26, and retreat to a nearby Mexican restaurant. But for most of the day, Sheralyn Richardson of NPF was an indomitable spirit, cheering on each runner in her loudest voice, even when most of the others had retreated to the restaurant. By the time I reached them, near the five-hour mark, they were soaked, exhausted, and hoarse from cheering. But they still greeted me with a huge wave of enthusiasm. It felt so good to give my wife and daughter a hug before heading for the finish of my fourth consecutive L.A. Marathon, crossing the line in just under 5 hours. For the first time I had run solo throughout the race. I knew I couldn't keep up with Tom Dean and the pace group he led for the Honda Running Club, and I didn't want to keep him from helping the others get under the four-hour mark. So I ran alone, yet not really alone, because I was running for Honda, and for Team Parkinson. After finishing, I stopped by the Honda hospitality room. Once again I was greeted with applause from teammates, a warm towel to dry off with, and people eager to get me whatever I wanted. How could anyone be so lucky to have been a part of such a great day in L.A., in the company of so many friends, and to work for such a great corporation? I felt very blessed.

Just over four hours later, after the thousands of runners had passed, the skies had darkened into night, and the wind stiffened; after the street sweepers swept through and cars returned to the streets, Mary Yost finally made it to the Team Parkinson Cheering Station. She and her nephew, Tom Provost, had kept walking through nine hours of the worst weather in Los Angeles history. They finished the complete marathon in 9 hours, 18 minutes, and received their finisher medals alone in the dark of night. Mary became my hero forever. Not only had she conquered the L.A. Marathon in spite of her Parkinson's, she had done it in the toughest conditions imaginable. And Team Parkinson raised nearly $50,000. Our premier fundraiser that first year was Kathleen Cooper-Burton.

I was out of town during the wrap-up luncheon a few weeks later, but Edna said it was very emotional and positive. The first effort by Team Parkinson would have to be called a success by any standard. But there were a couple of burnouts along the way, including Tom and Mignone, both overloaded with the work they'd taken on for the Team. Sadly, they were not to be seen the next year, nor were Kathleen Cooper-Burton and several others from Mignone's Orange County chapter of the NPF. But new people stepped up to take their places, including Edna, who became chairperson for the event in its second year. Carol Walton still directed most decisions, and provided much of the support from the Alliance offices in New Jersey, but many new faces joined the team, and contributed to its success. As far as I know, Mary Yost and I were the only participants with PD who completed the L.A. Marathon in the first year of Team Parkinson. But as a result of our effort, and the effort of the entire Team, we raised the level of expectation for others.

In L.A. Marathon XVI at least 3 finishers ran the 26.2 miles in spite of Parkinson's disease: Nick Camonte, Florence Woolery and me. It may not sound like much, but that's a fifty-percent increase over a year earlier! Oddly enough I didn't learn about either Florence or Nick until after the marathon, in fact, never even met them until months later. I was very busy at work before the race, and I had to leave all the Team Parkinson's preparation in Edna's hands. I was struggling just to keep up with my responsibilities at work while trying to maintain my fitness. I wasn't training as much as I should have, and I didn't even talk to anyone else from Team Parkinson. I was feeling isolated and a little depressed again. I needed some support, and found it just a month before the marathon when I met Mark Saxonberg at an industry meeting in Las Vegas. Mark works for Honda's most important competitor, Toyota, as a manager in their Service Division. I'd been looking for a running partner, and someone at the meeting told me Mark was a good runner. I needed a workout, so I left him a business card, and asked him to call me. We got together early the next morning and ran 7 or 8 miles. As we ran, I told Mark what I was doing with Team Parkinson, and our preparation for the L.A. Marathon. He seemed interested, so we set up a time to run the following weekend—a big 18.6-mile run at Hansen Dam, one of those major tune-up runs before the marathon, put on by the L.A. Roadrunners and Students Run L.A. The principle behind it: "if you can get through this, you can do the marathon." Mark hadn't been training for any event in particular, but he was fit, and certainly not afraid of a challenge. Running over 18 miles at a ten-minute-mile pace gives you lots of time to get to know someone, and I liked what I learned about Mark. He's a small, strong runner with curly, graying hair and beard, not overtly muscular, but with a solid build, and probably a little younger than I was. One of those guys who knows his own mind, speaks his piece, and leaves it up to you to decide whether he's right or not. You get the feeling he's not asking for your agreement; he just wants you to know how he feels about the subject. Not arrogant or egotistical, just a little blunt.

Eighteen miles is a long way. I struggled a little, and got very tired, but I already knew I could do another marathon. Mark just seemed to breeze through it. I think in a way it may have actually energized him. Though the marathon was just three weeks away, he decided to run it with me. I was thrilled and relieved because I knew I was going to need some support along the way.

Just two weeks before the race, Edna got a call from a young woman who asked how she could run for Team Parkinson. Her name was Patricia Skeriotis. She had trained for the marathon for several months, and then stopped in January when she got hurt. But after a few weeks of rest, she was eager to run again, and wanted to commit herself to a cause—a friend referred her to Team Parkinson. As she and Edna talked, she decided she not only wanted to run the event for the team, she wanted to run with Mark and me. I was skeptical. She sounded like someone just wanting to do a marathon for a good cause, and Parkinson's disease sounded like a good cause. I didn't mind her running for the team, but I didn't want to be slowed down by a first-time runner who hadn't trained properly. A few days later Patricia came out to the strand at Hermosa Beach, and joined Mark and me on a ten-mile run. She seemed to have no trouble staying with our pace, and turned out to be very determined as well, so we agreed that she should run with us. During the marathon in L.A., she struggled in the middle miles, and I struggled near the finish. In the end, I had to admit I leaned on her as much as she did on me. And we both leaned on Mark. He was everywhere during the race, talking to Patricia about her acting career, exhorting the crowds to "get excited and make some noise," occasionally circling back to talk to children along the roadside, and periodically running off to high-five someone in the crowd. Yet he was always there alongside when we needed him. He proved to be solid and reliable, like running alongside the Rock of Gibraltar. The race had been a struggle for me because while Patricia labored through miles 15 to 20 we lost a lot of time, and I got further and further out of balance in my medications. My running became very erratic. From mile 20 on, Patricia got more and more determined, as if she could smell the finish line. She was going to see it through. I hadn't counted on being out there so many hours, and had to limp weakly into the Team Parkinson Cheering Station and beg for a little boost of Sinemet. After a kiss from my wife, a hug from my kids, and a tablet or two of essential drugs, we were ready to carry on to the finish. The three of us, Mark, Patricia and I, finished together in 5 hours, 38 minutes with our hands clasped together and held high. After that run, Mark and I started training together regularly. Patricia had achieved her goal, and decided that was enough. Mary Yost (who had walked the complete marathon the year before) and her son Colin acted as support crew for Colin's wife, Moana, running her first marathon. She finished in less than 5 hours!

We raised over $60,000 that year, and sent all of it to The Parkinson Alliance to be directed specifically at funding new research on Parkinson's disease. Because of its unique role in the Parkinson's community, and its financial support from the Tuchman Foundation, The Parkinson Alliance promises every dollar of individual donations will go directly to support research. The Alliance works with all the Parkinson's disease groups, and does not get bogged down in the territorial disputes that sometime fracture the community. There are many different needs in the Parkinson's community, and many organizations have been formed to deal with the different aspects of patient services, caregiver support, and scientific research. But many well-intentioned organizations often compete with each other for recognition and funding. Fortunately for Team Parkinson, our relationship with the New York Unity Walk and our support from The Parkinson Alliance keeps us out of such conflicts.

Our top fundraisers that year were Daniel and Jean Marcus, two members of Mignone's Orange County group who stayed involved with Team Parkinson. I didn't get to know them the first year or even before the second year's race because I was so busy at work, and training for the race. I finally met them at the team's first "carbo-load dinner" the night before our second Team Parkinson marathon. Daniel was in his 60s, and had been diagnosed with PD about five years earlier. He had also been blind for several years from *retinitis pigmentosa*. He liked the idea of being in the marathon, and was able to arrange with the L.A. Marathon Committee for him and his wheelchair to be pushed the last six miles by six of his caregivers and family. They carried a large "Team Parkinson" sign, and wore our team T-shirts. In the race, they got a lot of attention. Daniel always had a warm smile on his face, and though he couldn't see them, he had a way of responding to the cheering crowds that they could feel—he connected with them not with pity or pain, but with joy.

Jean was incredible at acquiring and organizing the things Daniel needed to stay engaged with life. She and Daniel stayed active even through his deepening illness, and were constantly surrounded by family and friends. They even vacationed on a cruise ship, making lots of new friends along the way. They had no qualms about asking people to support Daniel and Team Parkinson, and Daniel made it so easy because he was genuinely pleasant, and fun to be around. No wonder they became such great fundraisers!

As the second year of Team Parkinson was wrapping up, Edna agreed to stay on as chairperson for the marathon. So, with a seasoned veteran in charge of efforts for L.A., Carol Walton felt free to delegate much more responsibility to the local Parkinson's community. Edna poured her heart and soul into Team Parkinson for 2002, and added several new features to it. She struggled to develop a website, and forced herself to learn new computer skills in the process. She also formed several sub-committees responsible for individual elements of the event. Planning the "Carbo-Load Dinner" was a big responsibility, because it combined pre-race festivities, team-building, and dinner, with recognition of the fundraisers. Dana Schneider was asked to head up the dinner sub-committee, allowing Carol and Edna to focus on writing their presentations for that evening. They had to thank an enormous list of people, and they wanted to give recognition to the athletes as much as the fundraisers. We were also treated to brief presentations by Dr. Michael Jakowec, a researcher at USC, and Dr. Marie-Francoise Chesselet, head of the neurological research center at UCLA. They described how grass-roots efforts like ours provide the initial financing of "seed grants" that allow them the opportunity to secure much larger grants from the National Institutes of Health. The focus of much of the Parkinson's research in their institutions is directly related to finding a cure for the disease. It was exciting to hear that our homegrown fundraising efforts can be leveraged to make such a difference.

The top fundraiser for Team Parkinson in its third year was Aaron Moretzsky, a middle school vice-principal in the Los Angeles City Schools. Aaron joined Team Parkinson in its second year when students in his Pacoima Middle School chapter of Students

Run L.A. decided to raise money on his behalf. Imagine a vice-principal so well respected by his students that they decide to run the marathon in his honor, and then went out and collected over $2,000 for Team Parkinson! As an active member of the Team Parkinson steering committee, Aaron was able to bring greater visibility to our efforts. One of his former students, Mark Ridley-Thomas, then a councilman on the L.A. City Council, heard about Aaron's condition and his work with the team, and asked what he could do to help. Aaron casually suggested that some recognition for Team Parkinson might be in order. Ridley-Thomas put together a Proclamation, which he presented to Team Parkinson, and read into the official record of the L.A. City Council. The Proclamation acknowledged the contributions of Team Parkinson to society, and praised the example the team sets for community-based action. Edna made sure the core committee members of Team Parkinson were at the Council meeting to be acknowledged. Aaron Moretzsky, Mary Yost, Dana Schneider, Edna and I were all there with our special guest, May May Ali, to receive the Proclamation. None of us had ever been to a City Council meeting; it seemed totally disjointed and without any logical sequence. The whole affair was a little like visiting the Wizard of Oz—quite strange and marvelous.

May May Ali was, like Aaron and Dana, a second-year addition to the Team. She is the oldest daughter of Muhammad Ali, the heavyweight boxing champion who is undoubtedly the most widely recognized person on the planet living with Parkinson's disease. May May and her sister Laila agreed to be honorary co-captains of Team Parkinson in our second year. Their pictures on our brochure added a measure of recognition to our efforts. But over the next year she became an integral part of the team, providing a voice for Team Parkinson to the media. She learned about us in March of 2001 when Kim Seidman invited her to the team's carbo-load dinner the night before our second marathon. Edna had posted several of the local newspaper clippings we'd been able to generate, and May May read them all while waiting for the dinner to get underway. Later, when she was introduced to the Team, she said she was so inspired by our efforts, both fund-raising and running, that she promised to run the next one with me. She said she would like to train with me, and get in shape for the event. Of course it wasn't the first time I'd heard such promises. My son David had been similarly "inspired" after my finishing the marathon the year before, but nothing had come of it.

We kept in touch with her during the following year, but May May never seemed to have time to train. I began to doubt she would keep her promise, but she pointed out that she had run two previous L.A. Marathons on her own, and hadn't trained for either one. I asked her how she could do it without training. She smiled and said, "It's in the genes." Considering what a magnificent athlete her father was, I couldn't argue. As the marathon approached, her commitment to Team Parkinson became more visible. She not only intended to run the marathon for the team, but she was also ready to help whenever we had opportunities with the press. I can tell you that she is certainly not a publicity-hound. In fact, quite the opposite. Too many people see her as a way to get close to her famous father, so she normally tries to remain out of the limelight, while still trying to pursue a life connected to the theater and entertainment business. She's caught in a contradiction of goals and ideals, trying not to cash-in on her father's celebrity, while trying to launch a career of her own in the arts. In her daytime life, she has a full-time job as a caseworker with at-risk students in the L.A. City Schools. In fact, she almost didn't make it to the City Council meeting because she didn't want to skip work. We were happy to have her with us since she's easily recognized as her father's daughter, and the media are eager to get close to any celebrity.

After the success of her presence at the City Council meeting, we asked May May to join us at the L.A. Marathon media luncheon. I'd been invited before, but on my first visit I felt more like a spectator than a participant. The second time I understood a lot more. Honda and the L.A. Marathon set up the luncheon as an opportunity for the press to meet key people from the field of runners who will not be at the front of the elite group, but have a story to tell. For example, the oldest runner in the field, 89-year-old Ernie Van Leeuwen, was sitting next to the youngest competitor, a nine year-old girl who was walking the marathon with her mother. I was there because I was running in spite of Parkinson's disease.

The luncheon is Dr. Bill Burke's opportunity to show the L.A. media how the L.A. Marathon and the City of Los Angeles work together to bring honor to the community and inspiration to its people. Dr. Burke is the President of the L.A. Marathon and essentially owns the event. He's quite a character, and loves telling stories, and being in the spotlight. On my third trip to the Media Luncheon I was able to arrange a couple of interviews with journalists from local newspapers. It certainly felt great just to be included in the event. But when I brought May May along, we became the center of attention for a while. Burke is a long-time friend of her father. In fact, he claims to remember seeing May May as a tiny baby. She was proof, he said, that God has a sense of humor, because she was probably the ugliest baby he'd ever seen, and yet here she was, a beautiful young woman, almost as beautiful as her daddy. Because of Bill Burke's attention to her, she drew the attention of the press to Team Parkinson.

All that attention nearly overshadowed the guest of honor at the luncheon. Each year, Burke tells the story of Patsy Choco's effort to run the L.A. Marathon in spite of terminal cancer. He reads the letter she wrote, asking for permission to have her husband meet her with a wheel chair to help her across the finish line if she couldn't make it on her own. He tells the same story each year, but it doesn't get any easier. It is truly a heart-wrenching story of courage and ultimate tragedy, and it has the power to turn the room to tears. I think he was moved even more deeply that year than the two previous years I attended. In fact, he couldn't even finish reading the letter. After telling Patsy's story, he eventually recovered his composure, but only because Patsy's husband and daughter were both there to help him give the Patsy Choco Courage Award to Jackie Joyner Kersee. Kersee is the most successful woman track and field athlete in American history. She has won gold medals in at least three different Olympic Games, and in several events. Her last Olympic gold medal was a dramatic come-from-behind win in the long jump, after which she retired from competition. She was given the Patsy Choco Award not because of her success in the Olympics, but because she has worked so hard to make a difference in her hometown community of East St. Louis, Missouri. She also dedicates her time as a motivational speaker for Students Run L.A. She is not only an outstanding athlete, but a concerned social activist as well.

After lunch and all the speeches and the award to Kersee, May May Ali still gathered much of the attention of the press, particularly the photographers. Since we were there as a team, I was asked to stand on the platform with her while photographers circled us like sharks, and writers shouted questions at us. That was far more attention than I'm used to, and I was feeling uneasy because of it. The added stress escalated my Parkinson's symptoms to the point that I became very uncomfortable and twitchy. Eventually Jackie Kersee was brought in to join us for the photographs, almost as an afterthought. What a strange feeling, being sandwiched between the world's greatest woman track athlete and the daughter of the "greatest of all time!"

When questions from the press naturally led to questions about her father's Parkinson's disease, May May was quick to point out she was running the marathon for Team Parkinson, not just for her father. She even suggested her father might have something to learn from some of our team members about handling his medications and staying fit. She's suggested more than once that her father doesn't pay enough attention to how his medications are working, or how to use them effectively.

On race day, May May also played an important role for Team Parkinson by helping Moses Remedios finish his first marathon. Moses found out about Team Parkinson just three weeks before the 2002 L.A. Marathon. After receiving our flyer in the mail, he called Edna to find out more about the team, and to pledge his support to our fundraising efforts. While they were chatting, he mentioned that he had thought occasionally about running a marathon, but now that he'd been diagnosed with PD, it didn't seem that it would ever happen. Edna told him about my plans to run L.A. for the seventh year in a row. He was bowled over by the possibility that his fate really wasn't predetermined. The realization choked him up, and then reduced him to tears! Edna tried to console him, but he interrupted her to say that these tears were not from sorrow but from joy. He hadn't even considered the possibility of being in the thick of things after 20 years with Parkinson's. At 33, Moses thought all the good times were behind him, and he'd been contributing to this downward spiral through self-destructive behavior. The notion of running the L.A. Marathon caught his imagination, and fired a few dopamine-diminished synapses. After the phone conversation, Edna couldn't get him off her mind. She called him back and arranged a meeting between us.

We met, and we decided to go for a run to see just where he was physically. He looked quite good really, still working out regularly in the gym, and running on the treadmill, although he hadn't run in the streets. We ran nearly ten miles that morning, just two weeks before the marathon, and I encouraged him to trust his instincts. If he thought he could run a marathon, then there was nothing in this world that could stop him, other than himself. A few days later, he joined our workout group led by Mark Saxonberg, and ran another ten-mile workout. I could tell he was struggling a little on that second run, but I wasn't sure whether the struggle was to keep up with the pace, or to fully grasp the idea of running a complete marathon. I gave him all the encouragement I could, but I wasn't certain he believed me, or believed enough in himself.

Although Moses was a little late, he did make it to the carbo-load dinner the night before the race. He walked in just as Edna was telling the emotional story of how Moses found Team Parkinson, and about the tears and the possibilities, and that he was committed to running the marathon. It was interesting to see the effect Moses had on other young-onset Parkinsonians. I don't think any of them realized how many young fellow sufferers were out there, nor did they have any collective idea what the future holds for them. Normally, when they attend a support group meeting or a conference on Parkinson's, they're likely to be surrounded by people in their sixties, seventies and eighties. The problems facing those older people are very different from those facing young-onset patients. Older patients look for tips on how to safely get out of bed, or from the bed to a wheelchair. The young-onset patient is more concerned with questions about marriage and children and careers. It's challenging for them to watch the slow, faltering steps and tentative balance of their older counterparts. But on the night of the Team Parkinson dinner, the marathon, the bike ride, and the 5k bring us together. It's a chance to think about the possibilities their lives present, not the limitations. The young-onset group was looking at older, yet more fit, examples of people living with PD like Jim Wetherell and Ted Bean in the Bike Tour, and me in the marathon, and they were reassessing their potential.

On race day, Moses joined us in the hotel lobby before the race. He was ready to run, though not quite sure what to do next. I was there with Edna, my training partner Mark Saxonberg, and my kids, David and Sarah who were running their first marathon, just like Moses. Two years earlier, David had promised to run the next marathon with me, but nothing came of it, except another promise. Sarah, on the other hand, had said nothing at all, but went back to school in San Francisco and began running on her own. She trained regularly for months, and then finally called David and asked how his training was going. He said he was going to start sometime soon. She surprised him by asking if he would run with her. He was unaware she had any plans to run, and had always believed his sister was unatheletic. She had never even run a 5k! She talked him into running nine miles with her, and he really trashed his body in the process. He had to rethink his assumptions about his little sister. After that, they trained together for the few weeks remaining before the marathon. Sarah joined Mark and me on our last run before the marathon, and had done pretty well up to about 11 miles, and then she struggled for the last two. I just hoped they were ready.

We jogged off together to join the thousands of runners stacked up behind the starting line, and waited for the sound of Randy Newman singing *I Love L.A.* to proclaim the start of the race. But an unexplained delay developed, grew longer and longer, and everyone grew more and more fidgety. And everyone kept drinking water to avoid dehydration later on, making some even more uncomfortable, but no available restrooms could possibly have accommodated even a fraction of the 22,000 packed side-by-side in the street, there was no place to "go." I got very tired just standing around, using up my dopamine resources faster than if I'd been running. I could see that Moses was also uncomfortable, but I wasn't sure whether he just needed a bathroom break, or was concerned with the thought of trying to keep up with Mark and me. In the end I simply told him, "Run your own race."

When the gun finally sounded, and 22,000 people surged forward, we all separated and eventually lost sight of each other in the crowd. My kids dropped back while Saxonberg and I took off at a comfortable pace. Before long, Mark dropped back to take a quick bathroom break. I spotted May May in the crowd, and then Moses joined us. Mark caught up a minute or two later, and the four of us ran a few blocks together. Mark and I wanted to move along faster than the others, and as we moved away, May May decided to stick with Moses. They stayed together, and helped each other throughout the entire race.

Along the way they decided to have a good time! They stopped for a coffee break at Starbuck's; and grabbed a snack at a mini-mart along the way; and even had their photo taken together under a large billboard of May May's dad. The billboard announces AliProject. com, a new website, dedicated to Parkinson's disease information. They finished together in 6 hours, 37 minutes. A couple of weeks later, May May introduced her new friend Moses to her father Muhammad.

David and Sarah were both successful in their first run at the distance, and even finished side-by-side, well ahead of Moses and May May, but about 30 minutes behind Mark and me. They did a great job, especially when you consider Sarah had never been in a race of any length before that day, and their training schedule had been so short. I hope eventually we can all run a marathon together, but I'm really looking forward to the time when they can leave me in the dust!

In 2002, Team Parkinson was a bigger success than we had even hoped for. We raised more than $90,000 in our third year, and runners from other parts of the country took notice of our efforts. Merging two things as incongruous as Parkinson's disease and running a marathon has a certain power to draw participants and spectators to the challenge of the race, a metaphor for conquering the disease. And a marathon, because it's such a large-scale event in most cities, can provide a broad venue for raising both money and awareness. After great success in our third year, I believed Team Parkinson was poised for growth. After we became the first official charity of the Culver City Western Hemisphere Marathon for November 2002, we decided to expand Team Parkinson beyond Los Angeles.[18] With the expansion in mind, Edna suggested I become her co-chair for the event, thus doubling our resources.

---

[18] For reasons having nothing to do with Team Parkinson, the Western Hemisphere Marathon was later cancelled for 2002.

Chapter 14
Other Transitions

Dr. Waters left USC Medical Center in June 2000 for a new position at Columbia University Hospital in New York City, so I began seeing her associate, Dr. Lew. About the same time, the USC neurology center added some staff, including a new group doing primate research. Things were also changing at work. I'd been managing the technical training department for nearly 15 years, and in that time, the responsibilities had grown significantly. The automobile market in America had become Honda's largest, and our department had assumed responsibility for supporting the Central and South American Honda distributors as well as the entire U.S. market. The job had grown beyond my ability to manage it successfully. So in March of 2000 my boss acted on his earlier promise to find me a place to contribute, and split the job three ways. This created a new position for me called the Industry/Education Coordinator. My new challenge was to develop partnerships between Honda and automotive educational institutions to increase the number of qualified technicians available to Honda dealerships. There's a severe shortage of technicians in the retail service business, so manufacturers and automotive service organizations are working on ways to attract bright, capable young people into the trade. My goals would be to strengthen Honda's support for vocational programs, and set up long-term strategies for developing more technicians in the future. I'd no longer have to manage 15 staff members, and direct the efforts of 30 field instructors. The stress in my life was significantly reduced, but my PD symptoms didn't seem to get the message.

After serving as Industry/Education Coordinator for about two years, I decided to take another step back from my day-to-day work. A traffic accident in December of 2001 made me realize I was putting other people at risk by pushing too hard day-in and day-out. I'm happy to put myself at risk when the possibilities for success seem worth it, but what can be worth putting others at risk without their consent? I tried to minimize the risk by joining a car pool, and letting others do the driving. But too often my schedule didn't match the car pool schedule, or didn't allow me the flexibility to do my own driving or come in late or leave early when I knew the effects of my medications could be minimized. After commuting from Whittier to Torrance for 25 years, I knew it was time to relinquish my slot in the car pool lane, and give up my spot in the parking lot. I told the management team at work I had decided to leave. Afterward, there have been several times I wanted to revise or withdraw that decision.

I retired from American Honda in May 2002, a really tough decision for several reasons. First, the value of my 401(k) plan was dropping steeply with the descending stock market. All the money I'd put in for the previous two or three years had evaporated. Second, the projects I was working on were long-term, large-scale efforts that couldn't be wrapped up by my retirement date. Third, I was working with the boards of several education-related organizations concerned with improving education for automotive technicians, and the terms of my commitment to them didn't automatically end on my retirement date. Fourth, I couldn't imagine not working each day in the company of friends, and I feared losing touch with them. Fifth, I didn't want to give up running with the Honda Running Club at lunchtime, and riding my bike on Wednesday evenings with the Honda Bike Club!

The company alleviated many of my concerns. They couldn't fix the stock market, but they did agree to support my continuing participation in the Board positions I held, and to engage my services as a consultant in my area of expertise, technical education and training. My boss also asked Edna for a twenty-year "kitchen pass" for our Wednesday night bike rides, sort of a "get out of jail free" card entitling me to join my riding buddies for dinner after the ride. Perhaps the most important support I have from Honda is the smiles I see on people's faces when I walk back into the building in my shorts and tee shirt "retirement uniform." Whether I'm there to work or to play, it feels good either way. What more could a guy ask for? I felt like the luckiest man alive.

When I left Honda in May of 2002, I told people I had two goals in my retirement. First, I wanted to be more active in helping people with Parkinson's, and also helping my wife by serving as co-chair of Team Parkinson. Second, I wanted to continue contributing to the growth of technical education in North America. I suppose many of them thought I would simply go home, kick back, and rest on my laurels. Of course that was always a possibility, but it hasn't turned out that way at all. Instead I went from one full-time job at Honda to another full-time job at home. From a job I knew well, to a new job where all the responsibilities were in flux. I'd always thought working full-time at Honda while training to run the marathon was really tough, but running Team Parkinson turned out to be much tougher.

Chapter 15

Learning to Succeed

When I agreed to co-chair Team Parkinson, I figured I'd have more than enough time to help out. After all, Edna was chairperson for two years while still taking care of her dad, and working 20-25 hours a week as a librarian. But I didn't consider the effect of the Team being in expansion mode! In three years we had raised $50,000, then $60,000, and finally $90,000 per year. The number of people involved had gradually increased as well, but in the fourth year, they seemed to expand exponentially. Membership was increasing locally and also spreading into other markets. A runner from Houston named Gabriel Zamora decided to raise money for Team Parkinson by running the Suzuki Rock and Roll Marathon in San Diego in June of 2002. He wanted to honor his father who had Parkinson's disease. His efforts raised $10,000 for our team. Then in the fall of the same year, Jonathon Schancupp decided to raise money for Team Parkinson at the New York City Marathon to honor a friend's father, who also suffers from Parkinson's. Donors responded with more than $5,000. A few weeks later, we headed in a new direction. May May Ali put together a night of entertainment at the Comedy Store in Hollywood to benefit Team Parkinson. She lined up the facility, and got the comedians to contribute their performance to support the fundraiser. We gave out lots of complimentary tickets to make sure we'd be playing to a full house, but the evening still brought in over $4,000. Some of the comedians seemed to ignore our pleas to use only their "clean" material, but it was a truly hilarious evening of entertainment.

Word of Team Parkinson was spreading beyond L.A., but each step into a new arena brought additional work to our team at home. All too often Edna was up at 5 o'clock each morning to begin answering e-mail traffic from the East Coast, and wouldn't shut down for the night until 10:30 or 11. Our biggest 2002 fundraiser, Aaron Moretzsky, continued coming up with new ways to garner support. He wrote solicitation letters to all the car dealers and Wal-Mart stores in his neighborhood and beyond, as well as many charitable foundations. Eventually some of them responded, dealership-by-dealership, store-by-store. One Wal-Mart store chipped in $50; another sent a check for $100, while two other stores came through with $1,000 each.

Between January and March of 2003, incoming mail for Team Parkinson went from a trickle to a flood. Edna kept up day-to-day communications with Carol and Terri Hamran at the Alliance office in New Jersey, and I tried to take care of web site maintenance. Edna had originally designed our site using an off-the-shelf product from Microsoft, but Gloria Hansen, the new webmaster for the Alliance, decided it would run better, and display more consistently across the web if it were constructed with HTML tools instead. Then the Alliance decided to install new software to allow secure on-line donations, and our simple, one-page, homespun site was transformed into a large-scale, third-party-managed affair. Now members of Team Parkinson could set up their own home page within the site, and declare and track their personal fundraising goals. We could now send group e-mails and run individual reports. The upgrade scared off some of our less computer-savvy team members, but I tried, with limited success, to coach a few more experienced members into setting up their own pages. The possibility of getting on-line donations seemed unlikely at first, because most of our donations are responses to the solicitation letters members send to their friends. But over the next few months, on-line donations steadily increased. This year we included a pre-printed return mail envelope with our letters, making it much easier to credit the donation to the correct team member. With the return mailers, the on-line donations, and the constant flow of emails from Edna to the team, we began to see a dramatic increase in donations. Since Edna was still working part-time at the library, much of my time was spent driving the loop from our house to the post office to the Fed Ex office and back.

Along the way, Edna and I were constantly reaching out to potential new Team members, hoping to engage them in our fundraising activities. Even the L.A. Marathon Committee decided to expand its support of its Official Charities by hosting an on-line auction just before L.A. XVIII. Although this outreach activity brought new revenues to Team Parkinson, it also expanded the workload. Instead of lightening Edna's workload, my becoming Team co-chair had simply expanded our expectations! Between the two of us, we decided to raise our target from the $90,000 donated in 2002 to $125,000 for 2003. We couldn't really say exactly how this would happen, but we felt certain it could because we had an "angel" looking out for us: Daniel Marcus.

After Daniel's wheelchair-ride in the 2001 marathon, he had set a new target for himself and Jean. He wanted to be pushed the last ten miles of the marathon by ten beautiful women, and raise ten thousand dollars for Team Parkinson. But as the 2002 L.A. Marathon approached, Daniel's condition worsened. Although too ill to make the journey, he never gave up his desire to be there. Even in the hospital, nearing the end, he asked Jean to keep his running shoes under his bed just in case. Daniel died just a few weeks after L.A. Marathon XVII, and Team Parkinson dedicated its efforts for 2003 to honor his memory. At our carbo-load dinner, Jean had his running shoes with her as she spoke to the team about Daniel's passion for the marathon. Later, Carol and Edna presented Jean with a medal to wear as a necklace. It was inscribed on one side "To the memory of Daniel Marcus," and on the other side with an image of winged running shoes. We knew our angel Daniel would be watching over us.

Whatever our expectations, they couldn't possibly have matched the reality of Team Parkinson for 2003. Due to the diligence of everyone on the team, we shot past our fund-raising goal a couple of weeks before the race, and money continued to stream in for weeks afterward. By the end of the campaign, we had received over $170,000, exceeding our goal by nearly $50,000!

The fund-raising was a tremendous success, but I think even greater success was achieved by our team members in the bike ride, the 5k run and the marathon. Forty-five runners and walkers completed the 5k for the team, and thirty runners and walkers took to the streets for the L.A. Marathon wearing the colors of Team Parkinson. All thirty starters finished, many for the first time, including Ken Aidekman, co-founder of the Unity Walk in New York, and an original member of the planning group at Mary Yost's apartment in December 1999. Ken had ridden a bike in the Acura Bike Tour for the first three years of Team Parkinson, but he was so inspired by our success that he decided to run the marathon.

In an email to Team Parkinson after the 2003 event, Ken wrote:

> *Of course I had ulterior motives for participating in the L.A. Marathon. If you've ever been in Northern New Jersey during February you know how appealing the idea of flying to L.A. in early March can be! Then there's the exercise. I've thoroughly enjoyed riding in the bikeathon for the last three years. I bought myself a bicycle to train for the first ride, and since then the bikeathon keeps me motivated to work out and stay in shape. But this year I'm going for the whole enchilada – the marathon itself.*
>
> *When I first learned there were people with Parkinson's running in the marathon, I was astounded. John Ball is my hero. Two years ago May May Ali announced at our carbo-loading dinner, "If John Ball can run the marathon, I can, too." When she finished the marathon last year with a smile on her face I said, "If May May Ali can run the marathon, I can, too." Unfortunately, someone actually heard me say it, and it was suddenly too late to back down; the cat was out of the bag.*

I've never doubted Ken's sincerity in support of Team Parkinson, but I wondered if he would find training for the marathon to his liking, especially through a cold New Jersey winter. Each time I talked to him he seemed to have problems with his feet, his knees, his ankles, and so on. I had my doubts. But on race day, Ken was right there, passing the Team Parkinson cheering section at mile 26 in a quick jog, and far earlier than I would have expected. We were all surprised, but proud of him. I think his desire to run, instead of walk, past his teammates was almost too much for his tired legs because he came to a sudden stop just beyond the Team Parkinson supporters. He was frozen in place with cramps in both legs. Mark Saxonberg and I went to help him and, after a few minutes of careful massage, he was able to move on. While we worked on his legs, I was tempted to tease him about trying to show off, but I just couldn't . . .his determination had earned our respect.

We were proud of all the first-timers, especially those running to honor loved ones with Parkinson's. And we were especially proud of two new marathoners with PD who managed to go the distance. David Schneider was in his second year with Team Parkinson and in the fourth year since his diagnosis. In 2002, David came all the way from Japan to be part of the team, and to walk the 5k with his wife. His sister Dana and mother Betty Sancier had walked the marathon that year with Mary Yost, who was attempting her second marathon.[19] In 2003, David moved up to the big-time. He trained in Japan for several months before coming to L.A., and knew he would have the support of his family when he got here. On race day, David, Dana and their mother Betty set off at a brisk walk at the back of the pack. Unlike many walkers, they had the good sense not to push forward into the crowd at the start, and become a hazard to the runners behind them. Since Dana and Betty were veterans, they knew what to expect, and walked just fast enough to stay ahead of the street sweepers and closing water stations. All three of them—David and his sister and 73-year-old mother—finished in good health in 8 hours, 36 minutes.

---

[19] Due to the long delay at the start and the heat of the day, Mary was forced to drop out of LA XVII at the 17-mile mark.

Just a few minutes behind them were Steve and Stella Evans, a brother-sister team from Washington State. Steve was diagnosed with PD in 1985. He decided soon after he was not going to simply give up on himself, and he started running to keep his strength up. In spite of his efforts to stay fit, he lost a great deal of his physical capabilities over the next 17 years, until, in 2002, he finally decided to undergo brain surgery to implant electronic probes in both sides of his brain. Deep brain stimulation (DBS) surgery, available for just the last five or six years, essentially replaces earlier surgical techniques such as pallidotomy and thalamotomy. Instead of making permanent lesions in the brain, DBS surgery implants one or two small electrodes deep in the sub-thalamic nucleus near the base of the brain, and the implants produce small electric pulses to control the excess brain activity associated with Parkinson's disease. DBS is proving successful at reducing the side effects of medications, as well as reducing the overall impact of Parkinson's on the patient. In Steve Evan's case, after living with PD for nearly two decades, he felt sufficiently improved by DBS that he decided to run the marathon only 7 months after the surgery.

Steve wrote:

I had been corresponding with Edna and John Ball for about 6 months. They're the heads of TEAM PARKINSON L.A. and in charge of handling the donations (my sister and I collected almost $2500.) They were at the convention center when we went to the Team Parkinson booth and introduced ourselves. We all got hugs from Edna, and they all seemed genuinely glad to see us. Carol Walton and Ken Aidekman were there too. They're on the Board of the Parkinson Alliance, and had flown in from New Jersey. The Parkinson Alliance gets the funds from TEAM PARKINSON L.A., which is in turn matched dollar-for-dollar by the Tuchman Foundation. It's complicated, but ultimately it means all the money collected goes directly to research, 100% of it!

Anyway, they all seemed intent on the idea that I was going to make history. THE FIRST DBS PATIENT TO

*SUCCESSFULLY COMPLETE A MARATHON! NO
PRESSURE THERE! They expected me to finish but my
knees had been bothering me for about two months. In fact I
hadn't exercised at all for two weeks before leaving, hoping
my knees would be repaired enough to at least walk it. I was
taking Ibuprofen in big doses. Could I do it? I had my doubts
but I would at least attempt it. What was I getting into?*

*Saturday was pretty uneventful. We just hung around
the hotel, resting up for Sunday. I was taking my Ibuprofen.
Sue got bored and walked down to the Convention Center
again to pick up some souvenirs. That night though, we went
to the Team Parkinson L.A. Carbo Load dinner. About 100
people there. Many were support people. Some planning to
do the Bike race and some the 5K walk, two other races they
run with the marathon. The room was filled with excitement
and anticipation. There were speeches about commitment
and dedication, and everyone seemed genuinely interested.
The doctor who does the research, and is the recipient of
the money also talked. Seemed very optimistic. Then came
my big thrill. May May Ali was there! Muhammad Ali's
daughter...in the same room! I finally got her free for just
a moment and shared my story about the torch run and how
her dad had inspired me when he lit the cauldron in Atlanta.
I also got my picture taken with her. How about that! She
was friendly and bubbly and full of personality, and looked
just like her dad. We really enjoyed ourselves. Next stop the
Marathon!*

*A perfect day. Sunshine and about 60 degrees. I was up
at 4:00 AM. My blood was pumping. The race didn't start
'til 8:30. I drank a few cups of coffee, and ate the muffin
and milk I ordered from room service the night before. Sue
was blissfully sleeping, so I just watched TV and drank
my coffee. My clothes were all laid out. My hat...singlet...
race number...shoes and socks...sun block...sunglasses...
Vaseline...power cells...muscle balm...Ibuprofen...etc. I was
dressed and ready by six.*

Wait...Wait.... Wait.... 6:15.... Wait.... Wait...Wait ...6:30...
Wait...Wait...Wait...7:00.

Sue got up and got dressed. At 7:30 we went downstairs for
pictures. We met up with the other runners, had our pictures
taken, and then the excitement really started building. We
started walking toward the starting line. The sunshine, the
warm air, downtown L.A. with its buildings reaching up to
the blue sky. It was impressive. I could feel the excitement
in the air as the sound system blared out. Runners were
everywhere! My sister and I positioned ourselves at the back
of the crowd so as not to get in the way of the faster runners.
We intended to walk it, if my knees held out. I had pain in
my knees at the starting line. The first aid station was at
seven miles. If the pain increased, I could bail out there. If
it stayed the same I would continue. These thoughts were
going through my mind as we stood waiting. I didn't want to
cause any permanent damage.

We're off! As we cross the starting line the crowd on
the side of the road is cheering. I'm feeling good. Even if I
only go 7 miles it'll be worth it. I'm in the L.A. Marathon!
The 4TH largest in the world! And I'm here because of an
amazing surgery. If I couldn't finish, it wasn't important. It
was the journey that brought me here that counted. But in
the back of my mind I told myself I was going to try, and try
hard. I walked past the cheering people, and there was May
May, Muhammad's daughter! She sees me! She waves! What
a thrill.

The first two miles took us about an hour because of
the crowded start, but after that we were stepping out pretty
good. The pain in my knees was still there, but not getting
any worse. So I was feeling comfortable. We went through the
next three miles without any difficulty, and then it happened.
The clean up crews were moving up on us, and we were told
to move to the sidewalks. Not only that but they were closing
down the water stations just before we reached them. We
could be in serious trouble...walking on cement and stepping

up and down curbs for twenty miles can be taxing; not only that, but water and Gatorade are crucial. We managed to get water at the water stations from a few of the volunteers that saved some cups after the trucks roared through. A few times we managed to get the last two cups. There were still people behind us! I don't know what they did for water. Walking on the sidewalks was dangerous. Many were old and narrow and uneven, with the slab edges sticking up. We would walk out in the streets for a while but the trucks would move up on us and we would once again retreat to the sidewalks. We fought the trucks for the next fifteen miles. From sidewalk to road and back. Trying to find water before they cleaned up the water stations. We got to only one station before the trucks did, at mile 16. Griping about the water and dodging the trucks kept us pretty busy. My knees? What knees? They didn't hurt at all now! About mile 13 I felt like I was really going to do it. In fact, I was really doing it. It's downhill from here!

That's the way it went till mile 18. Leap-frogging with the cleanup crews, scrounging for water and off and on the sidewalks. We were still about 8 miles away when they opened the streets to traffic. And then we had to walk on the sidewalks only. By mile 20 the sidewalks started taking their toll, we began to get blisters, and both of us were hobbling a bit. We found an aid station where they treated our feet, and we were off again.

Because the roads were opened up we were afraid of taking a wrong turn somewhere and getting lost, but there were others in front of us, and we just hoped they knew where they were going. The miles were slowly ticking down...21...22... 23...At MILE 24 we passed a man who was 85 doing his 19TH marathon.... At MILE 25 we passed a young man on crutches who was dragging his spindly legs as he pushed toward his goal. I felt guilty for complaining about my blisters...Then MILE 26, and there were my Team Parkinson people patiently waiting more than 8 hours for *our appearance. Edna and Carol ran out to meet us and gave us each a hug. I was going to make it. Sue ran over to me and said she was proud of me. Two tenths of a mile to go! I CAN'T STOP NOW. We turned the corner and there it was—THE FINISH!*

As I walked through the finish I checked my time: 8 hours and 40 minutes. There in front of me was a young lady with a medal to put around my neck, and as I lowered my head, I thought to myself: "I earned this!" I now have that medal on my wall, along with my singlet and my number.

I finished this trip with no regrets. It started as a dream I've had for a long time –to complete a marathon. I started training for it last July. Exactly one month after surgery. It's been an interesting road. I'm 53 and have had DBS surgery. There aren't many books on how to train so I had to go by feel much of the way. I originally planned to run it, but maybe next time. How are the knees? Haven't hurt since MILE 7.

Finishing the L.A. Marathon is not only a first for Steve; it must be a first for medical science. I'm certain the Parkinson's community across the country will be both surprised and elated to learn of his triumph.[20]

My own marathon run was much better in 2003 than the year before. Mark Saxonberg and I had trained together on weekend long runs ever since we met in Las Vegas, just before the second Team Parkinson effort. We ran with Patricia Skeriotis that year (2001), and the three of us took over 5-1/2 hours to finish. But in our second effort (2002), I messed up my medication schedule, and struggled through what should have been an easy run for both of us. Mark was in great shape, and I wasn't far off, but I ate some gel food concentrate before I took my medications at about mile 11, and my performance deteriorated continuously from there on. The gel has the ability to be picked up easily by the bloodstream, which meant it completely

---

[20] Steve's complete account of his incredible journey through the L.A. Marathon XVIII weekend can be found on the Team Parkinson web site at: www.teamparkinsonla.org.

blocked the uptake of my medications. I was terribly dyskinetic, wobbling all over the road, and each step was a forced effort. I had to hold on to Mark's arm, or around his neck, just to keep moving forward. Mark ushered me into the medical tent at the finish, and I spent several minutes on the table, receiving fluids intravenously. I recovered quickly after the extra fluid got my medication circulating. Two weeks later, Mark ran the Catalina Marathon in good time, and I was able to meet him on the trail at mile 22 and bring him in to the finish. Mark was really rounding into great shape, and began planning to add other marathons to his schedule.

Gradually over the next year, Mark had encouraged other runners to join us, and by the time the L.A. Marathon arrived in 2003, we were a team of five. Stacey Lashley, Mike Harmon and Doug MacGlashen had all committed to the training, and to Team Parkinson. It was the first marathon for Stacey and Doug, the second for Mike. On race day we added two runners who hadn't trained with the group. Bill Curry, Carol Walton's brother, from Seattle, and Ann Eckles from Monrovia joined us as well. I don't think either Ann or Bill had trained as hard as our local team, but they made a go of it nonetheless. Bill hung with us until Mile 13 then dropped back suddenly—he had a sore calf, and didn't want to hold us up. Mark circled back to find him but he said to go on. Ann just kept pressing on until Mile 19 when she really "hit the wall." We had to decide whether to stay together or run the race we'd planned. Mark, Mike, Doug, Stacey and I were all doing well. In fact, I was feeling better than I had in several months. I'd finally sorted out my medications, and realized that by trying to compensate for the emotional stress of the day I had been overmedicating. On this race day I kept my dosage to the minimum I normally lived with, and it worked much better. I made it to Mile 10 on my first dose for the day, and I then took my regular dose at around 10:30, just half an hour earlier than normal.

We had held back through the first half of the race, hitting the ½ marathon mark at 2:32, and we then held back even more, arriving at Mile 20 about five minutes under the 4-hour mark. We wanted to "let it all hang out" for the last six miles, but we could see Ann wouldn't be able to stay with us. So, do we go as planned, or stay together as a team? Since our name was Team Parkinson, not *Time* Parkinson, we decided to stay together. We finished six across, with our hands together and held high above our heads. A truly wonderful experience; I'm glad that we did it that way. I think the whole team agreed.

Team Parkinson fielded a trio of first-timers with Parkinson's in the 5k walk as well. Bruce Wisnicki's personal story is similar to that of Michael J. Fox. They're about the same age, were married about the same time, and actually met while on their honeymoons in the same hotel! They were both diagnosed with Parkinson's disease in their early thirties. Each also attempted to deny the disease to themselves and the world around them for some time. They just wanted to be free to pursue family and career concerns like everyone else. And they each had the tenacity to continue in their careers in spite of the disease. Bruce has been successful in his career in the financial business while Michael was extremely successful in his acting career. Also like Michael J. Fox, Bruce Wisnicki had been looking for an opportunity to contribute to the Parkinson's community. He had worked closely with researchers at both UCLA and USC, and supported their efforts financially. In 2003, he joined Team Parkinson's fundraising efforts. With his family to support him, he also chose to walk his first 5k. He and his family succeeded in both efforts. Bruce, another first-timer with PD, walked the 5k with daughter Julia while his wife Kathy ran with son Jake. They too worked hard, and became our biggest single-family fundraisers, boosting our total by over $40,000.

Jim Wilber also walked his first 5k for Team Parkinson in 2003. Jim is in his 60s, and having lived with Parkinson's for years, had lost a lot of mobility, as well as much of his voice, facial expression, and handwriting ability, losses common to many PD sufferers. When he joined Team Parkinson, Jim decided to call everyone in his church directory to ask for a donation. He's part of a large church congregation in Camarillo, California, and this turned out to be a formidable task for someone who'd lost most of his voice. He was determined to make the effort, and kept at it day-after-day, eventually raising over $4,000, much of it in $10 and $20 donations from members of the church. He called hundreds of families in the weeks before the marathon, and in the process, his voice strengthened and his interest in things grew. He talked his son into running the 5k for him, and then talked himself into walking it. Since Jim hadn't been able to walk without a walker or cane for some time, his wife Dorrie was concerned at first, then decided to walk with him to make sure he would be all right.

After the marathon weekend, Jim's son wrote:

My Dad has had PD since 1985, and it has become an effort lately to do the things we used to do so easily. Just getting in and out of a car can be a big ordeal. But somehow our experiences with Team Parkinson for the carbo-load dinner Saturday and at the L.A. Marathon/5K Sunday seemed to go so smoothly. It was as if we went through a time warp back in the past to a time when everything was not so difficult. It was incredible to be with so many nice people who understood what my family and I have gone through for the past 18 years, to share our experiences, and have fun all at the same time. If all this wasn't good enough already, I ended up getting my personal best time in the 5K run with a 22:30. I am so happy that my Dad found you guys...

Dr. Martin Polonski, Ph.D., had quietly been part of Team Parkinson for three years, but in 2003 at the suggestion of his neurologist, Dr. Giselle Petzinger, he decided to walk the 5k. Living with Parkinson's for many years reduced Marty's ability to walk, drive, speak and write. He can't easily drive to visit people, his voice is hard to hear over the phone, and his handwriting is unreadable. Without his computer and email, this gregarious, well-educated man would be almost completely isolated by PD. Dr. Petzinger was familiar with Marty's history of back and leg problems that had kept him in a wheelchair two years earlier. And she knew about the collapsing knee that often caused him to fall. But when she told him he might be able to walk the 5k for Team Parkinson, it gave him such a boost in confidence he was willing to give it a shot. He trained for months by walking laps around the local high school track, and then, in the last week before the race, he took to the roads and hills around his house. He got a little uneasy as his training progressed. It was such an odd feeling to be in fear of a simple three mile walk, when as a kid he had run 10k races with ease. Of course, as a kid, everything was possible, and he didn't think about limits. Now, after years of PD, he had to struggle to free himself from those limits.

On race day, Marty set off with the large contingent from Team Parkinson. Going at his own slow pace, he soon felt isolated, and narrowed his focus from watching the crowds down to simply finishing the event. Near the end of the walk, Marty tripped over some trash in the road and fell near the curb. Two nurses quickly came over to help him, and then, unexpectedly, Dr. Petzinger appeared and immediately took charge. She helped Marty to his feet, answered his ringing cell phone, and walked arm-in-arm with him the rest of the way. She'd been walking the 5k with her husband, Dr. Michael Jakowec, and their three kids under five years old. They were alternately towing and carrying the kids as they each popped in and out of the stroller. In spite of her own concerns, Dr. Petzinger decided that since she had started Marty on this journey, they would finish it together!

Another success that year was Edna and I being able to delegate some responsibilities to other Team members. Besides May May spearheading the Comedy event, Mark Saxonberg took over leadership of the training program for runners, and Dana Schneider supervised the entire carbo-load dinner. We were also able to considerably expand our "home territory." We added several new members from other communities within California, including the Bay area, and attracted runners and walkers from as far away as Washington State and Japan. I learned it's much more difficult to delegate responsibilities in a volunteer organization than in one of the departments of a corporation, but we're gradually learning what's appropriate to delegate, and what isn't. We've also learned not to expect too much from those of us with PD. At times our bodies simply will not be able to keep up with the goals we set for ourselves.

On the down side, we didn't succeed in developing a sub-committee for public relations, an area where neither Edna nor I feel comfortable. Perhaps the lack of a strong PR effort keeps us from drawing a more diverse membership. Certainly the L.A. Marathon draws its runners from a very diverse population, and yet we've not found a way to reach the Latino, Asian or African-American communities, and get them excited about Team Parkinson. So, there's much more work to be done to bring the Team to the level where it can make a serious difference in the funding of Parkinson's research, but Edna and I have committed ourselves to the effort.

Chapter 16

Growing the Concept of Team Parkinson

Just three months after every L.A. Marathon, San Diego hosts a large, city-supported event, called the Suzuki Rock and Roll Marathon. Team Parkinson was represented there in 2002 by Gabriel Zamora from Houston, Texas. Gabriel had run with a few of his friends, and raised about $10,000 for Team Parkinson. His fund-raising had all come from his home area in Texas. He wasn't interested in running San Diego again in 2003, but Carol, Edna and I got a terrific response from several people in the San Diego area during our preparations for L.A., so we felt it was another opportunity to expand our Team. I thought it would be easy, since San Diego was close enough so we could work with team members there face to face when we needed to, yet far enough away to give them room to grow. And I thought it would be a good opportunity for me to run another marathon without losing the level of readiness I'd reached in L.A. With only three months separating the two races, I planned to train lightly during the week, and run long each weekend with Mark and the team. Both assumptions proved to be overestimates.

The people from San Diego who had been so enthusiastic in L.A. found they were caught up in the day-to-day routine once they got home. One by one they dropped the idea of running the San Diego race, and then gave up on fundraising, and finally stopped even planning to attend the carbo-load dinner. And I found it was all too easy to slough off the weekday workouts while counting on those long runs with Mark, Doug and Mike to maintain my fitness. After all, I was still floating on a cloud from L.A. It felt good to sit back and cruise for a little while. Edna and I were so thrilled with the success of L.A. that we couldn't stop smiling at each other for a month. But I kept taking days off from training. Mark had backed off training after hurting his knee, and Edna and I had been traveling a lot. We took a nice drive up to Bend, Oregon to see Tom and Connie Dean, and also made a four-day trip to New York City for the Parkinson's Unity Walk—The Parkinson Alliance helped us cover expenses so we could represent Team Parkinson there. Finally, I looked at the calendar and realized that the San Diego race was less than a month away, and I was definitely not ready to Rock and Roll. I tried to jam two-month's worth of training into the last three weeks before the race. I ran six, eight and ten milers over a four-day stretch, and then came back after two days with a 12 miler. Meanwhile, John Colvin, who had run L.A. for Team Parkinson, and was eager to do San Diego, called with two weeks to go to say he'd hurt himself and was dropping out.

Mark's knee injury was slow to come around, and he had eased back on his training. And Mark, Mike, and Doug had been very busy at work, and missed a few of the shorter runs they'd planned. On the positive side, after Doug's success at L.A., his wife Mimi had taken up running, and was preparing for her first half-marathon. Stacey was spending most of her time in the Bay Area, where she was training, but somewhat casually. Just two weeks before the San Diego race, Mark, Doug, Mike, and I got together for a 20-miler, and a week later ran a half-marathon with Mimi on Memorial Day. I was happy with my race, but even happier for Mimi, who ran the 13.1 miles in under 2:15, five minutes faster than my first half-marathon! Then Saturday, the day before the marathon, Mark and Doug took Mike out for a run, and ran him into the ground. They had nothing to lose because they would both be on their way to Japan the next morning. Mike, who had planned to run the second half of Sunday's marathon with me, became quite ill after the hard Saturday workout. So, after all was said and done, I ran a solo marathon for the first time since Team Parkinson started four years ago.

Of course, I wasn't really running "solo" because, as always, I had terrific family support, and because Carol, representing The Parkinson Alliance, came out from New Jersey to support our team. Besides, I was surrounded by hundreds, even thousands of runners, most of them wearing the colors of Team-in-Training (or TNT as they now call themselves.). Nearly half the 20,000 people who signed up for the San Diego Rock and Roll Marathon were members of Team-in-Training, and came from TNT chapters all over the country. TNT, a non-profit charity like Team Parkinson, uses the marathon to raise money for the Leukemia and Lymphoma Society. The difference between their organization and ours is more than simply scale, however, since they commit each runner who trains with them to a fixed target for fundraising. In return, TNT provides an excellent training program, including coaching, travel arrangements and entry into a key big-city marathon like San Diego. To do all that takes a big staff of professionals and volunteers, at considerable expense. Team Parkinson has been an all-volunteer effort so far, with no permanent staff. We try to minimize our expenses to maximize the value of the money we raise for research. We want all of it to reach the people working on a cure for Parkinson's disease.

Our carbo-load dinner on Saturday night before the race was a small affair, almost like having dinner with my own personal rooting section. There was Edna, and my parents, along with Carol Walton (our mentor, and Executive Director of The Parkinson Alliance) and my former high school track coach, Dick Sweet. Imagine the novelty of coming home to San Diego 41 years after graduating from high school, and still being able to enjoy the company of my high school coach! As far as he knows, I'm the only one from the track team still running regularly, or at least competing in marathons. I don't know if it's more accurate to say I run *in spite* of my Parkinson's disease, or *because* of it.

As Carol and Edna and I walked from our hotel to dinner in Old Town, we were stopped by two men on the street, one of whom had been diagnosed with Parkinson's disease about a year earlier. They were coming from the restaurant where we were headed, and had overheard some discussion about tomorrow's marathon. They acknowledged our Team Parkinson T-shirts, and were curious about the connection between Parkinson's and the marathon. We talked briefly about our mission, gave them one of our business cards, and the man with PD promised to get in touch. He seemed genuinely interested in starting a running program to improve his fitness, and wanted to join us at our next event. He's already followed up with an email to Team Parkinson.

Dinner was excellent, the company superb, and before long, I was ready for bed. Unlike L.A., the San Diego Marathon gets off to a very early start, which is probably a little tough for its primary entertainment—most of the rock-and-roll bands that line the course probably didn't go to bed between their Saturday night gigs and their Sunday morning marathon engagements. Some of them sounded a little ragged, but they were out there on the street, playing as early as 6 am. I got up about 5 am, and Edna drove me over to the start area. Because of the marathon, San Diego was in a perpetual traffic jam from 5 am to well past noon. I kissed Edna goodbye at the bottom of Laurel Street, and walked up the hill to Sixth, near the entrance to Balboa Park. As a kid, that park, including the zoo, was one of my favorite places to be in the world.

As race time drew near, I lined up well back of the starting line in my pace group, back with the slowpokes. I go with the five-hour guys now; not the four-hour guys like a few years back. After the gun sounded, it took me eight minutes to get to the start line. It was a very different feeling from the L.A. Marathon, very laid-back, almost unemotional, and yet I could see that even among the five-hour hopefuls, there were many well-trained runners. The weather was perfect, overcast and cool for June, and the bits of conversation I heard were usually about the hard work most everyone had put in to get ready. People seemed amazingly focused and confident. Even the obvious neophytes seemed certain they would finish. Although it didn't have the celebrity air that surrounds the L.A. Marathon, I did see Bill Walton standing among, and above, the crowd near the starting line. He's a local product, and attended the same high school my older brother did. He looked a little "weathered" for someone who graduated from high school five years after I did.

I ran the first several miles at a comfortable pace, not wanting to push myself hard too early, but without Mark alongside constantly checking the clock, I just let the walk and run intervals happen as they might. I did notice my tendency was to shorten the walk and lengthen the run. By mile 10, I was running constant 10-minute miles, and probably getting a little ahead of myself. Then I saw Coach Sweet alongside the road cheering for me, and I wanted to go even faster. The crowd wasn't as big as L.A., but at times the entertainment was better. On the other hand, there were sections of the race along stretches of freeway, isolated from spectators and the bands—awfully dull places to run. Once past the halfway mark, we circled back toward Mission Bay and more residential communities, and the size of the crowd increased.

While the crowd seemed to be picking up enthusiasm, I was starting to unwind a little. It kept getting harder and harder to stay on or near the pace I'd planned, and then it hit me: I hadn't yet taken my mid-morning dose of medications! At mile 14 I finally stopped to take my Sinemet, Permax and Comtan. In the last five years, that was the farthest I'd ever run on one dose, but it took the next five miles for the medications to get back up to effective levels. Those were five tough miles—I lost about 10 minutes off my goal—but when I hit the 20-mile marker, I could feel the truth in the adage "the race doesn't start till mile 20!" My medications were working well once more, and I felt like running again, while many people all around me were running into "the wall." I must have passed a couple thousand runners in the next three or four miles. Even without trying to calculate my revised pace in my head, I knew I could finish in less than five hours. As good as I felt at mile 20, I suspected that there was still a "wall" waiting for me somewhere before the finish. So just to be on the safe side, I backed off my pace from mile 24 on to the end, but still finished under 5 hours (4: 54). The finish was on the parade ground of the Marine Corps Recruit Depot, where I worked the summer of 1962 before leaving San Diego for college—a nice homecoming!

So, a great day for me, though not so great for Team Parkinson. We raised less money than expected, and had less of a presence in the race than planned, perhaps because the San Diego race is too close, both geographically and on the calendar, to Los Angeles. We certainly learned a lot from the San Diego experience, and also got to spend time with family, old friends, and our mentor, Carol Walton. Her normal visits are whirlwinds of activity that leave little time to relax, talk, and enjoy each other's company. On this trip, though, we had time to talk about the current Team Parkinson concept, and how it might change in the future. We learned a little more about what works and what doesn't, and about the commitment required of the local community to make out-of-town events successful. Overall, our visit to San Diego inspired us to continue exploring other races where Team Parkinson could be successful.

Chapter 17
One Tough Marathon

Because of the heat, the 2004 L.A. Marathon was a tough run for me, for my teammates, and just about everyone who set out to go the distance. And the heat of the day was just the immediate challenge. We had to overcome several unexpected obstacles in the months before the race just to get there. The previous year was almost magical by comparison. My teammates and I exceeded our goals in almost every category: more runners, more bike riders, more walkers, more events added to our calendar, and more money raised than ever before. It all seemed so easy. But this year, everything seemed difficult; we had lots of problems preparing for the marathon and for our fundraising event.

A year ago, I came into the L.A. Marathon better prepared than I'd been in three or four years. I'd trained regularly with Mark Saxonberg, Mike Harmon, Doug MacGlashan and Stacey Lashley. And we had stuck to a fairly rigid schedule of building distance runs at a 10-to-11-minute-per-mile pace over the course of several months. So on race day, we knew we were ready for a good marathon. We finished together, and we finished strong.

This year was very different. I took several weeks off from running during the summer while working in Detroit, writing a technical training proposal. The people I was working with were avid bike riders, so I joined them on several of their rides, both on and off-road. I hadn't done off-road riding in years, and it showed.

Some of the trails we rode were pretty twisty, and I was on and off the bike a lot, sometimes intentionally, sometimes not! On one of my tumbles I pulled some muscles in my abdomen. I fell hard, but got up and finished the ride, and later began taking pain relievers. Bike riding after that didn't hurt much because I was seated most of the time, but whenever I tried to run, my lower abdominal wall hurt . . . so I didn't do much running. The pain dragged on for several months. In October my doctor suggested heavy doses of Advil (800mg/3 times a day) for two solid weeks to bring down the inflammation. I followed his prescription, and the pain eased up somewhat, although it still hurt just turning over in bed at night.

In the meantime, Mark, Mike, and Doug were also suffering from various injuries, and Stacey had moved to San Francisco. Our plan to train year-round had collapsed. It was December before we really got back into a training frame of mind. Doug's wife Mimi replaced Stacey in our lineup, but the injury to Mike's Achilles' tendon was serious so he couldn't join us. My abdominal muscles had been slow to heal, and even five months after the incident still gave me considerable pain before and after running. I know runners are fond of saying "no pain, no gain" but for me it was "too much pain, no train." So I played catch-up with my partners all through January and February—they would wait for me at the top of each hill. Just two weeks before the race, I could stay within shouting distance of them most of the time. It was hard work, but after running nine marathons in the previous eight years, I knew I would eventually be strong enough to run this one. But that was only half the battle.

The other half was the fundraising work. Team Parkinson had grown a lot over the last two years. What began as a single race in L.A. became a sequence of events throughout the calendar and across the country. In this fiscal year, beginning June 1, 2003, we've already sponsored runners in major marathons in Chicago, San Francisco, Los Angeles and Napa Valley, and fielded a team of 23 runners and walkers at the U.S. half-marathon in San Francisco last October. We still have two events left: the Big Sur Marathon and Spokane's Bloomsday Run. And we've tried our hand at garage sales and dog walks!

As we filled in the calendar, our workload increased. Lucky for me, Edna is willing to handle almost all the detail work, including data entry, correspondence, tracking athletes and donations, collecting volunteers, and building team leaders for major tasks. She's marvelous at maintaining contact with our community of dedicated team members, vendors and volunteers. I try to help out by answering training questions, and encouraging those preparing to run, walk or ride. I also spend lots of time at the Post Office and the FedEx counter. As an Official Charity of the L.A. Marathon, we attended pre-race meetings with the L.A. Marathon Committee, and hosted a Team Parkinson booth for three days in the Quality of Life Expo.

There was one other factor that added some anxiety. I asked Laurence Cohen, media publicist for the L.A. Marathon, if he could help us boost the visibility of Team Parkinson. He did his best, and I became one of the "Saucony 26." The Saucony Shoe Company, a major sponsor of the L.A. and Boston marathons, had decided to help 26 mid-pack runners share their stories with the media, and promote their favorite charities. By representing Team Parkinson, I got to join a terrific group, ranging in age from nine to ninety-one, who all had special reasons for running the L.A. Marathon. Saucony displayed our images on eight-foot panels, and published our stories in a small book handed out at the Expo. We also did radio interviews before and after the marathon. It was a marvelous experience, but it did increase my stress while preparing for the race.

By race weekend, Edna and I were just about exhausted. We'd spent Thursday, Friday, and Saturday working the booth at the Expo as well as shuttling family and guests to and from our home and the airport. Saturday reached a crescendo of activity and stress as we prepared for the big carbo-load dinner that evening. Edna and I were the hosts, and for the second year in a row, I served as master of ceremonies. Fortunately, for the third year in a row, Dana Schneider had arranged the entire dinner in her usual professional manner. The restaurant staff seemed more courteous than ever, and the food even tasted better. The evening was a big success—good wine, good food, and a chance to share them with 100 of our closest friends! The audience included corporate sponsors from Boehringer-Ingelheim/ Pfizer and Novartis, medical and research staff from USC, California Neuroscience Institute, and all the athletes, supporters, family, and fundraisers.

Team Parkinson has been an all-volunteer effort from the beginning, and wouldn't have accomplished much without the tremendous support of our corporate sponsors, as well as the personal efforts of many friends. Edna gave special thanks to Kathy and Gerardo Martinez for their help at the garage sale, and for handling transportation during the marathon. She thanked Dana Schneider for the dinner arrangements and May May Ali for her book signing. I gave the athletes with Parkinson's special recognition—five of the nineteen team members in the marathon have PD. Gail Edgar and Jerry W [21] would each be attempting their first marathon. Gail, a 43-year-old who was diagnosed five years ago, learned of Team Parkinson at last spring's PAN conference in Washington, DC, and had trained entirely on her own. Jerry, our oldest marathoner at 73, was diagnosed less than a year ago, and has not yet told his friends that he has PD. He chose to remain invisible to other team members, and didn't attend the dinner. I mentioned my training partners, Mark, Doug, and Mimi, and also Bill Curry, Carol Walton's brother from Seattle, running his third marathon for the Team. Although he doesn't train with us, Bill's goal this year was to run and finish together with our group. Carol handed out the final bit of recognition to the "The Big A (sker)," Aaron Moretzsky, for once again being our top fundraiser, bringing in nearly $20,000. After dinner, Carol announced that Team Parkinson had raised $120,000 year-to-date, and there was still a major event on the calendar before June 30, the end of our fiscal year. Finally, the party ended—tomorrow morning is the marathon!

What can I say? It was hot at the start, about 70 degrees (F), and it got a lot hotter. The time and temperature sign at a local car dealership showed 90 + degrees (F) as we neared the finish line. At first I struggled for several miles, feeling under-medicated but trying to get some miles in before taking my next dose. At mile eight,

---

[21] Jerry remains in the closet with his PD.

dystonia hit my left foot, and I had to stop, take my medications, and wait for the spasm to release. Just the first stop of many for the team. By mile 11 or 12, Mimi was having sharp pains in her calves. From mile 14 on, we kept getting separated as she dropped back with leg cramps. We knew from cell-phone conversations that Carol and Gerardo were waiting for us at mile 15. Mark's wife Susan and son Jordan were waiting at mile 16, at the top of a small hill. With Mark encouraging us, we look incredibly fresh in the photos Jordan took there!

By mile 19, Mark and Doug had disappeared. Bill and I were walking together, keeping Mimi in sight behind us, and assuming Mark and Doug were ahead of us. I was certain they would eventually wait for us to catch up. Meanwhile, Mark and Doug assumed they had left us behind, and turned back to look for us. But . . . both assumptions were wrong! Mark went back at least a mile before concluding we couldn't be that far back—we had already crossed that point when he had last seen us. So he turned around again, ran to catch up with Doug, and the two of them ran on until they found Mimi, who was trailing Bill and me by about 50 yards. What a ragged quintet we turned out to be! Clearly, Mark was in the best shape, in spite of running an extra two miles. Bill could sustain a good walking pace, but was unable to bump it up to more than a shuffle. I could shuffle for brief periods, but didn't feel I could sustain it. So from mile 20 on, we settled for walking with 30-second shuffles every two minutes. It wasn't much of a pace, yet we were still passing people. When we finally reached the Team Parkinson cheering station at mile 25, Doug and Mimi had once again dropped back and were out of sight.

The three of us celebrated briefly with our teammates. We were more than an hour behind our normal pace, and it was extremely hot. We knew we could make it to the finish, but weren't sure we could still keep our promise to take care of each other, and finish together. Bill knew if he stopped and waited, he might not be able start again, so he continued on at an easy walk. Mark and I circled back, found Doug and Mimi, and brought them in to our cheering station. After a few hugs and kisses, the four of us moved on toward the finish.

After turning from Olympic Boulevard onto Flower Street, we faced a half-mile of gradual climb. We could see Bill ahead, walking to the right side of the road, and we caught up with him as quickly as Mimi could go. But in the meantime, Bill had begun to seize up. He stopped to get some pain spray on his calves, but couldn't get restarted. He was "frozen" in place, as surely as if he had Parkinson's disease. Mark and I circled back again, wrapped our arms around his waist, and helped him move forward, step-by-step, until he could take over on his own. The race clock was approaching the 6-1/2 hour mark as we finally lined up across the street, held each other's raised hands, and crossed the finish line. We had kept our promise and achieved both goals: we took care of each other, and we finished together.

Other goals were achieved as well. All five team members with PD finished the 26.2 miles, raising the total to nine in the five years of our participation in L.A. In the 5k run, the presence of fifty-five bright blue T-shirts with the Team Parkinson logo up front and our web address on the back, helped us raise the level of awareness of Parkinson's disease in the L.A. community. And the money we raised will help scientists in their search for a cure. This marathon was hard, hot work, made more difficult because of our commitment to stick together. Finding a cure for Parkinson's disease hasn't proved any easier, but it's a challenge we still accept, and a goal we'll keep working together to achieve.

Fighting your way through a marathon is an effective metaphor for fighting Parkinson's disease. And finishing the race represents a resounding, though temporary, victory over the disabilities Parkinson's imposes, one that foreshadows the absolute victory of a cure. We believe there's a unique relationship between the marathon and the needs of the Parkinson's community. With the help of The Parkinson Alliance, we hope to develop a model for Team Parkinson that can be implemented at major marathons across the country. Thousands of people train for months to be ready to run those marathons on race day, people capable of making a commitment, and doing the hard work required to get to the finish line. Marathon runners understand that the really big challenges are worth the effort it takes to achieve them. That's the same kind of commitment and effort it will take to focus the attention of the scientific community on solving the puzzle of Parkinson's. It may be an intricate puzzle, but we know it's possible to solve, just as surely as we know someone with Parkinson's can run a marathon.

The scientific community has already announced its readiness to find a cure. In 1999 the National Institutes of Health and the National Institutes of Neurological Disease and Stroke published a five-year-plan for finding a cure for Parkinson's disease. Dr. Fishbach, then head of NIH, said "We can find the cure in 5 to 10 years." Since the scientists already believe it's possible, we as a society need only make the commitment to help them—that means funding it. Team Parkinson can help, because we've made the commitment, and are willing to do the hard work.

The understanding of Parkinson's disease has changed significantly in the last five years. It's November of 2004 as I write these closing lines to my story. More than five years have passed since Dr. Fishbach's proclamation, and there is still no cure for Parkinson's, nor have we discovered its cause. But I'm still hopeful the cause and cure may be discovered in my lifetime. The last five years *have* brought a better understanding of the disease and its treatment. Parkinson's is no longer considered simply a movement disorder. It can affect movement, thinking, and the autonomic nervous system in many subtle ways interfering with everything from heart rate, respiration, and perspiration, to urination and defecation. At USC and UCLA, Parkinson's is being studied and treated by teams of doctors with expertise in a broad range of specialties. As patients, we've also learned we have more control over the progression of this disease than we thought. Running, riding, hiking and all the things I love to do have kept me functioning and engaged in life for over 30 years with this disease. Now we have scientific evidence that our brains have more built-in repair capability than anyone imagined. My running has not only helped preserve the brain cells that are still undamaged, but has probably helped repair many thousands more, and may even have generated new ones in the areas damaged by Parkinson's disease. This repair capability is called neuroplasticity—among the doctors I see at USC my nickname is

"Mr. Neuroplasticity." I can't say that what I've done will work for everyone with Parkinson's, because the disease affects each of us in different ways. I can say that I wouldn't trade my life for anyone else's. I've been blessed with a wonderful family, marvelous friends, and the best medical care in the world. Life is good—bring it on!

Chapter 18
Blinding Flashes of the Obvious

Throughout this book I've included some personal discoveries to remind myself I passed this way for a reason, and to help anyone who might be passing through a similar experience. I categorize many of these discoveries under the heading: "Blinding Flashes of the Obvious." We use lots of acronyms at work, so I just call them "my BFO's".

1. **Most problems with other people usually originate within me, not them. The same is true for the solutions to those problems. The way to change the world is to change myself.** This may seem so obvious that you wonder how I ever missed it, but for me, only the most extreme circumstances made me aware of it. For example, my refusal to accept a particular assignment in the Vietnam War resulted in anger, persecution, and hatred from my military superiors. I shouldn't have been surprised, since my refusal was based on a moral objection to certain conduct in that war. By objecting, I was attacking the foundation of their belief that we were morally superior to our enemies. Without that belief, it would be difficult for any sane and moral person to send their sons and daughters off to fight. I had to learn that the only way to get my superiors to treat my views with respect was to grant them similar respect for their beliefs. Since it's one of those lessons easily forgotten, it must sometimes be relearned the hard way.

2. **It doesn't make sense to finish everything you start. Some things are unhealthy for you.** This idea runs counter to conventional wisdom, and my basic nature. But the truth is, I would have been far better off taking Mike Carbuto's advice at my first Long Beach Half-Marathon, and stopped when I got tired. I really did hurt myself by trying to go the distance when I wasn't prepared for it. Fortunately, I was able to apply this lesson successfully when I first attempted to climb Mt. Whitney. This one is still difficult for me to apply consistently.

3. **When the chips are down, focus on solving one problem at a time, in order of their importance. Solve each problem the best you can at the moment, then move on.** This lesson was clearly defined for me as the result of a fire in the cockpit of a C-47 flying between Djakarta and Singapore. It's had many other applications at home and in business since then. I've found it to be one of the most important rules for helping other people succeed. I had to discover for myself that you must not assign all the toughest tasks to your top performers. Too many tasks at the same time can turn even the most successful people into failures. They may *want* all the tough assignments, but that almost guarantees some won't be finished on time, or with the quality you need. Also, since you're only going to solve one problem at a time, it's important to know which to take care of first.

4. **Events are merely events; it is how we decide to deal with them that create their meaning or value.** No one has absolute control over the events in his life, but each of us is responsible for making sense of those events and for finding something good or useful that might come of them. Bad events in your life may happen unexpectedly but it's up to you to choose between being victimized by them or victorious over them.

5. **Listen to your doctors, your family, and friends, but decide for yourself what you can or cannot do.** You are in the best position to know yourself. Before I had learned to apply this lesson, I gave up my pilot's license without a fight. I sold my motorcycle. I stopped trying to be "the best" at everything. I

could just as easily have given up on myself. The doctor said, "You have Parkinson's disease. You can't fly airplanes, and you can't ride motorcycles anymore." I should have asked, "Why? Are these decisions based on a concern for my welfare, or the welfare of others? These limitations may have been appropriate for others with this disease, but does that mean they must necessarily apply to me? Or are they simply an attempt to exert control over my 'I can do anything' attitude?" In the future, I'll be unlikely to accept the judgment of others without reviewing all the circumstances for myself. I can do lots of things in spite of living with Parkinson's disease, including fly airplanes and ride motorcycles, if I'm willing to make appropriate adjustments.

6. **We're unlikely to succeed at everything we try, but lack of success does not equal failure.** It's only failure if we fail to learn something from the experience. I probably learned more from not finishing my first climb on Mt. Whitney than I did from finishing that first Long Beach half-marathon. Every experience has the potential to teach you something, if you're prepared to learn. It's not enough to simply pile up experiences. Experience is really valuable only when it teaches you something new, something you can apply in new situations, or use to solve new problems. A corollary to this principle is that if you succeed at everything you try, you've probably set your sights too low.

7. **Life gets more enjoyable when you stop worrying about what you can't do, and focus on what you can do.** No one is much interested in why things are impossible. They're far more interested in what was accomplished in spite of significant difficulties. I once met the cyclist/pilot who flew the Gossamer Condor to win the Kramer Prize for man-powered flight. His name is Bryan Allen. The aircraft he powered and flew all by himself was a flimsy, transparent contraption of carbon fiber and Mylar that looked like it should collapse of its own weight. He powered the aircraft by continuously pedaling a bicycle sprocket while simultaneously controlling the aircraft from takeoff to landing. Eventually he was able to pedal a similar airplane from Crete to mainland Greece, duplicating the mythological flight

of Icarus (who flew too near the sun and melted his wings) and Daedalus (who stayed within the flight envelope and escaped the Labyrinth.) Someone asked him what the limit is for man-powered flight, and he answered, "The limit is our lack of imagination."

8. **No matter how alone you think you are, or wish to be, nor how much you may want to face your challenges alone, none of us is really flying solo.** Medical challenges like PD are community diseases. They affect not only the patient, but caregivers, family members, business associates, and friends. Our society has been slow to recognize that people with disabilities and chronic disease have special needs. We still have a lot to learn about how best to help each other. But with appropriate help from those around us, we need not withdraw from everyday activities. We have to learn to accept help when we need it, and give help when we can. The advent of the World Wide Web has significantly changed the way patients can help each other and work together. Support groups are fine for some people when the group can reach a critical mass, but with the Web, huge groups can form anywhere around any subject in almost no time at all. This has significantly increased the rate of learning and distribution of knowledge. It has also broadened our concept of "community."

9. **Finding the "balance" between our expectations and our true potential is the key to feeling good about life.** This is life's high-wire act, and for me the higher the better! It's part of aging, as well as an adjustment to a disease process. We all will come to a point, for whatever reason, where we can no longer expect improvement in our performance. How does the high achiever know when to back off, or the underachiever learn to stretch? If you set a target you have the capacity to achieve, but you don't really believe you can achieve it, your effort will be wasted, and your wounds self-inflicted. A decision to risk it all is most likely to succeed if it's inspired by the core values that define who you believe you *should* be, not by what you are now or were in the past.

10. **If you think something is impossible, it is, until somebody else does it.** In high school we believed several critical pieces of false information. For example, our belief that runners shouldn't drink water while running may have put us in danger of dehydration. We didn't believe anyone in high school could run a mile in less than four minutes, or run a marathon. Believing these things made them true. By the time we found out they were false, the opportunities they denied us were gone.

11. **Strength and fitness can overcome lots of challenges.** In fact, strength and fitness are probably the two most important tools in your toolkit, whether or not you are facing chronic illness. Regular exercise maintains strength and fitness, which in turn promote a mental and physical toughness that helps us resist unhealthy pressures in the world around us. The goal? Physically strong enough, and mentally tough enough, to be reliable under everyday pressures.

12. **Most of the things I've done in life got done only because I was willing to work hard at them.** As a kid, I was lazy and I don't remember having specific goals. I simply wanted to prove I could do things, but I didn't want to work at it. It wasn't until I began running that I learned the value of hard work on a particular goal. Some of the things I've done as an adult may be of value to someone in the future. For example, the system of training we developed at American Honda for technicians has proven very effective and may set the standard for technical training in the future. It would also be nice if Team Parkinson turned out to have played a part in finding a cure for PD. I'm willing to do whatever I can to see that through.

These 12 lessons are not the only things I've learned in life – though I learned them slowly and sometimes painfully – but they were lessons that have stayed with me and proven useful in a wide variety of situations. Some were learned by fighting for what I believed in during the Vietnam War, and many were learned in fighting my private war with Parkinson's. They've helped me get through marathons and many other challenges, but these were the lessons of the past, and they won't be enough for the future. We'll all need new lessons in the future, because I believe we're going to be "learning our living" from here on out. The world is changing at an accelerating rate and if we can't keep up with it, we'll surely get left behind.

I don't hold up my life as an example of triumph over impossible odds, because the odds are nearly always manageable if you marshal all your resources. My particular obstacles may be less than many people face every day. And my triumphs may seem trivial to those who have no interest in climbing mountains and running marathons. Any time I get to feeling too self-important, I have only to think about the young woman who passed me in the marathon running on her titanium leg, and it brings me back down to reality. But I've been able to lead a full life, raise a family, and work in a challenging job for 25 years *in spite of Parkinson's disease*. In the process, I feel I've learned a lot about what it takes to be a team player and a contributor in life. I've also learned that, with enough motivation, anyone can finish a marathon – and I do mean anyone! In 2003, a Viet Nam veteran *with no legs* completed the L.A. Marathon in 4 days by walking on his knuckles. Afterwards he said, "I may have lost my legs in the war, but I didn't lose my heart."

The Marathon is not the answer to any of life's most perplexing questions, nor is it a guide for how to live your life, because it's really a very simple idea, and life is terribly complex. It is just THE MARATHON—a 26-mile, 385-yard foot race. There are grander contests, but it is grand enough to define the difference between failure and success, victims and victors. The real winners are those who overcome each personal limitation to complete the journey . . . and learn something from it.

Appendix A
Team Parkinson Helps to Fund Exercise Grant at USC

In June of 2003, Team Parkinson was very pleased to be able to support Parkinson's disease research at the University of Southern California, Keck School of Medicine with a grant of $20,000. The grant money will assist USC's Department of Neurology to examine the value of exercise as a tool for strengthening the Central Nervous System's ability to adapt and reorganize in response to injury or disease. Team Parkinson is very interested in this particular study because it provides a scientific analysis of a phenomenon experienced by several of our team members: we seem to have better control over our Parkinson's symptoms while training aggressively for a particular event, like the 5k walk or the marathon. The doctors at USC believe that this regular exercise affects not only the Parkinson's symptoms but also causes permanent changes in the brain circuitry, enhancing cognition, mood and quality of life. Team Parkinson is proud to be able to support this research.

John Ball - Co-chair Team Parkinson

The effect of exercise on cognition, mood, and quality of life in Parkinson's disease

M. Welsh, J. Hui, C. McCleary, M. Lew

The central nervous system (CNS) has the well-known ability to adapt to changes in the environment by rearranging its circuitry. This CNS "plasticity" allows the brain to strengthen existing circuits, or compensate for damaged ones due to injury or disease. This project aims to study whether exercise in Parkinson's disease (PD) can induce a permanent rearrangement in brain circuitry, thereby improving cognition, mood, and quality of life. These circuitry changes have already been shown to occur in normal individuals, where regular aerobic exercise results in enhanced mood and executive cognitive functioning. These behavioral measures have further been associated with increased connections between neurons and greater brain tissue density.

In the proposed study, we will examine individuals with moderate stage Parkinson's disease. Participants will be randomized to an aerobic exercise program consisting of walking, a non-aerobic program consisting of stretching, or a control group, who will continue with their current activity level. The exercise groups will meet three times a week, and all participants will receive standard medical treatment for their PD symptoms. At the end of 6 months, exercise will be offered to all participants. Our outcome measures will include assessments of memory, executive planning ability, mood, anxiety, and perceived quality of life. We hope to be able to follow enrolled individuals for years to come, and document changes in cognition and mood over the course of the disease. In addition, we hope to obtain functional brain imaging at yearly intervals to document anatomic changes occurring as a result of the disease.

We believe that regular exercise in PD will cause a permanent rearrangement in brain circuitry, thereby enhancing cognition, mood, and quality of life in individuals with the disease. We hope to show this by measuring the effect of exercise on certain measures of brain function. The results of this study will be an important step in being able to alter the course of PD, perhaps as easily as prescribing exercise as an early intervention.

Appendix B

Team Parkinson is pleased to support USC's Department of Neurology Parkinson's study group. – June, 2004

Team Parkinson is pleased to support Dr. Michael Jakowec and his research team through the purchase of a ten-lane mouse treadmill. This device will help researchers to qualify and quantify physical outcomes for various drug therapies and treatment strategies in mouse models of Parkinson's disease. Dr. Jakowec suggested that all the mice that run on the treadmill will be called "John."

Enhanced Recovery Through Treadmill Exercise in the Mouse Model of Parkinson's Disease. – Dr. M. Jakowec

The brain's capacity for recovery from injury is far greater than previously recognized. Recent studies in a number of labs have shown that intrinsic neuroplasticity in either the non-injured or injured brain can be facilitated through activity-dependent processes including environmental enrichment, exercise, forced-use, and complex skills training. Interestingly, we are also learning that neuroplasticity is evident, not only in the young brain but persists, although less robustly, in the aged brain.

Most of our understanding of activity-dependent neuroplasticity is derived from studies focusing on the cortex and hippocampus especially in models of development, response to injury, and in learning and memory. There is now evidence that the phenomenon of enhanced neuroplasticity through exercise occurs in animal models of basal ganglia injury. In addition, studies in individuals with moderately severe Parkinson's disease provide compelling evidence that treadmill exercise improves functional level, ambulation velocity and endurance suggesting neuroplasticity.

A primary focus of our lab is to better understand neuroplasticity (and repair) in models of Parkinson's disease. Both the mouse and nonhuman primate, when subjected to the neurotoxicant MPTP (1-methyl-4-phenyl-1,2,3,6-tetrahydropyridine), which selectively destroys nigrostriatal dopaminergic neurons (the same neurons lost in Parkinson's disease), leads to behavioral and biochemical features similar to that seen in human PD. Remarkably, both the MPTP-lesioned mouse and nonhuman primate recover from the effects of MPTP but it takes a period of several months. Our goal is to find ways to enhance this natural recovery and by doing so identify new therapeutic modalities for the treatment of basal ganglia disorders including PD. In addition to pharmacological and molecular intervention strategies in the lab we are exploring we have also found that we are able enhance motor behavior deficits in MPTP-lesioned mice subjected to an intensive treadmill exercise program. Interestingly, our studies indicate that there are remarkable changes in those genes and proteins involved in dopamine neurotransmission as well as another neurotransmitter system that uses glutamate. These results have recently been published in Fisher et al (2004) Journal of Neuroscience Research 77: 378-390. Ongoing and future studies are designed to better understand the molecular mechanisms underlying exercise-enhanced recovery in the basal ganglia. For example, we wish to know how precisely the dopamine and glutamate systems are altered, and can we further enhance the benefits of exercise or even block them with pharmacological treatment targeting dopamine and glutamate. In addition, we wish to explore important questions regarding age-related benefits of exercise, how long the benefits persists, and if other tests of motor behavior enhancement are also affected by treadmill exercise.

To accomplish these goals we wish to add to our existing treadmill facilities for running mice. The addition of a new state-of-the-art treadmill will allow us to run additional numbers of mice in a shorter period of time, more accurately quantify behavioral measures, and allow computer integration of these measures. These mice would then act as a foundation for further investigation of the molecular, neurochemical, and behavioral mechanisms responsible for exercise enhanced recovery. By understanding these mechanisms in a mouse model of Parkinson's disease, similar studies applied to humans with Parkinson's disease can be designed and interpreted leading to improved patient treatment.

Appendix C

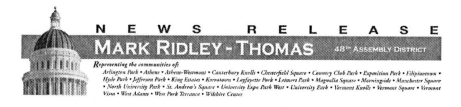

N E W S   R E L E A S E

MARK RIDLEY-THOMAS 48ᵀᴴ ASSEMBLY DISTRICT

Representing the communities of:
Arlington Park • Athens • Athens-Westmont • Canterbury Knolls • Chesterfield Square • Country Club Park • Exposition Park • Filipinotown • Hyde Park • Jefferson Park • King Estates • Koreatown • Layfayette Park • Leimert Park • Magnolia Square • Morningside • Manchester Square • North University Park • St. Andrew's Square • University Expo Park West • University Park • Vermont Knolls • Vermont Square • Vermont Vista • West Adams • West Park Terrance • Wilshire Center

FOR IMMEDIATE RELEASE
Friday, April 16, 2004

CONTACT: Missy Johnson
(916) 319-2048
Pager (916) 328-1014

RIDLEY-THOMAS TO HONOR TEAM PARKINSON

SACRAMENTO – On Monday, April 19th, Assemblyman **Mark Ridley-Thomas (D-Los Angeles)** will introduce representatives from Team Parkinson during Assembly Floor Session and acknowledge them for their fundraising efforts in the fight against Parkinson's disease. Team Parkinson is a non-profit organization committed to increasing public awareness on the impact of Parkinson's disease on society and raising money to fund scientific research required to find a cure.

"Team Parkinson has done an outstanding job in raising enormous amounts of money for Parkinson's disease research," said Assemblyman Ridley-Thomas. "Most of their members, some of whom have Parkinson's, have overcome tremendous physical challenges to compete in marathons to draw attention and funds in the fight against the disease. Team Parkinson's unwavering commitment to this cause is most impressive and is worthy of the Assembly's recognition."

John and Edna Ball, Team Parkinson Co-chairs and Aaron Moretzky, the organization's top fundraiser, will be acknowledged during Monday's Floor Session. Team Parkinson was created in 2000 and since that time has succeed in raising over $250,000 of which 100% of the net proceeds go directly to Parkinson's Disease research. Team Parkinson is the official charity of the Los Angeles Marathon and participates in races throughout the country to duplicate the Los Angeles success.

#####

Appendix D

Organizations and Resources for Parkinson's Disease Patients and Caregivers

American Parkinson Disease Association (APDA)
1250 Hylan Blvd.
Staten Island, New York 10305
Phone: (800) 223-2732
Fax: (718) 981-4399
Website: www.apdaparkinson.com
E-mail: apda@apdaparkinson.org

Michael J. Fox Foundation for Parkinson's Research (MJFF)
Chelsea Piers, Pier 62, Suite 305
New York, New York 10011
Phone: (212) 604-9182
And
1001 Pennsylvania Ave. NW
Washington, D.C. 20004
Phone: (202) 628-2079
Website: www.michaeljfox.org

National Parkinson's Foundation (NPF)
1501 NW Ninth Ave.
Bob Hope Rd.

Miami, Florida 33136
Phone: (305) 547-6666 toll free (800) 327-4545
Website: www.parkinson.org

Parkinson's Action Network
1025 Vermont Ave. NW Suite 1120
Washington, D.C. 20005
Phone: (202) 638-4101 toll free (800) 850-4726
Fax: (202) 638 7257
Website: www.parkinsonsaction.org
E-mail: info@parkinsonsaction.org

Parkinson's Disease Foundation (PDF)
710 West 168th St.
New York, New York 10032-9982
Phone: (212) 923-4700
Website: www.pdf.org
E-mail: info@pdf.org

Parkinson's Resource Organization (PRO)
74090 El Paseo Suite 102
Palm Desert, CA 92260-4135.
Phone: (760) 773-5628 toll free (877) 775-4111
Fax: (760) 773-5803)
Website: www.parkinsonsresource.org
E-mail: info@parkinsonsresource.org

Parkinson's Unity Walk
30 West 90 St.
New York, New York 10024
Phone: (212) 580-6505
Website: www.parkinsonwalk.org

Stem Cell Action Network
Portraits of Hope
Website: www.stemcellaction.org

Team Parkinson
6412 Broadway Ave.
Whittier, California 90606
Phone: (562) 692-8504 toll free (866) 822-CURE (2873)
Website: www.teamparkinsonla.org
Email: teamparkinson@hotmal.com

The Parkinson Alliance
PO Box 308
Kingston, New Jersey 08528
Phone: (800) 579-8440
Website: www.parkinsonalliance.net

The Parkinson's Institute
1170 Morse Ave.
Sunnyvale, California 94089-1605
Phone: (408) 734-2800
Website: www.parkinsonsinstitute.org

Worldwide Education for Movement Disorders (We Move)
204 West 84th Street
New York, New York 10024
Website: www.wemove.org

Websites of Interest for the Parkinson's Disease Community

The Parkinson Alliance
http://www.parkinsonalliance.net/

People Living with Parkinson's (PLWP)
http://www.plwp.org/

New Hope for Parkinsons
http://www.newhopeforparkinsons.com/

I Never Give Up.org
http://www.inevergiveup.org/

Grassroots Connection Online Neurological Advocacy
http:www.neuroguide.com/

Family Caregiver Alliance
http://www.caregiver.org/

The Parkinson Web at MGH
http://pdweb.mgh.harvard.edu/

We Move – Education & Awareness for Movement Disorders
http://www.wemove.org/

Appendix E
Bibliography and Selected Reading List

Blake-Krebs, Barbara, M.A. and Herman, Linda, M.L.S., *When Parkinson's Strikes Early: Voices, Choices, Resources and Treatments* (Alameda, CA, Hunter House Publishers, 2001)

Cooper, Pamela, *The American Marathon* (Syracuse University Press, Syracuse, New York, 1998)

Fixx, James F., *The Complete Book of Running* (Random House, New York, 1977)

Fox, Michael J., *Lucky Man: A Memoir* (New York, NY, Hyperion, 2002)

Galloway, Jeff, *Galloway's Book on Running* (Shelter Publications, Inc., Bolinas, CA, 1984)

Holden, Kathrynne, *Eat Well, Stay Well with Parkinson's Disease: A Nutrition Handbook for People with Parkinson's Disease* (Fort Collins, CO, Five Star Living, 2000)

Kondracke, Morton, *Saving Millie: Love, Politics, and Parkinson's Disease* (New York, NY, Public Affairs, 2001)

Langston, J. William, *The Case of the Frozen Addicts* (New York, NY, Vintage Books, 1996)

Lieberman, Abraham, MD, *Shaking Up Parkinson Disease: Fighting like a Tiger, Thinking Like a Fox* (Sudbury, MA: Jones and Bartlett Publishers, 2002) ISBN 0-7637-1866-1

Lightner, Patricia, *Parkinson's Disease and Me: Walking the Path* (Bloomington, IN, 1stBooks, 2003) ISBN 1-4033-9729-5

Newsom, Hal, *HOPE,* (Mercer Island, WA: Northwest Parkinson's Foundation, 2002) ISBN 0-9716841-0-3

Sandrock, Michael, *Running with the Legends* (Human Kinetics, Versa Press, USA, 1996) ISBN 0-87322-493-0

Waters, Cheryl H., MD, *Diagnosis and Management of Parkinson's Disease, 2nd Edition* (Los Angeles CA, University of Southern California, 1999)

About the Author

John Ball has been a runner all his life, but didn't take up the marathon until late. Since turning 50, he has completed 10 solo marathons and several team efforts. Ball plans to run at least one more marathon: the March 2005 Los Angeles Marathon will mark his 10th consecutive year in the event in spite of Parkinson's disease. He was diagnosed in 1983, at age 39.

Ball lives in southern California with his wife Edna and their Airedale terrier, Scrabble. He is an advocate for the Parkinson's Action Network, and enjoys opportunities to share his positive message with Parkinson's disease support groups around the country. John and Edna serve as the National Co-chairs of Team Parkinson.

John Ball, Learning Consultant, Whittier

In 1983, John was diagnosed with Parkinson's disease. In 1996, he ran his first marathon. This year he will run his ninth. His goal? To show those with Parkinson's that there are no limits to what can be accomplished, and to bring attention to the need for research and funding in the search for a cure.

Photo Courtesy of "Saucony 26" - March 2004